VICTORY THROUGH THE BLOOD

JUANITA FORD

Kingdom Builders
PUBLICATIONS

DEDICATION

I'd like to acknowledge God, our Father and the Lord Jesus Christ for empowering me to write this book because I know I could not have done it without Him. I thank my husband, Charles, the editors, Glenda Keith and Lauren Benjamin, the many people whose testimonies are included, and the members of the body of Christ who supported and prayed.

Juanita L. Ford

CONTENTS

PREFACE

I would like to share with you a very valuable moment in my life from my first book. It was the fuel that helped me to write this book.

On November 25, 1998, I had surgery for fibroid tumors on my uterus. When I was released from the hospital; I experienced something life-changing.

I was lying in bed listening to a series by Dr. Creflo A. Dollar, entitled "Anointed Because of the Blood." All of a sudden a baby formed in blood entered into my spirit and I rose up from the bed. This was my first day home from the hospital; so naturally, I was supposed to be very weak, but during this period I received much strength beyond my ability. My husband, who knew I should not have been walking around, came upstairs to check on me. He had been having trouble with his neck and the Spirit of the Lord told me to lay hands on him for healing and it happened instantly.

We had two other houseguests, a lady and a gentleman. The lady came upstairs. At first, she could not enter the room; it was as if she was restrained by the Spirit of God. It wasn't until I motioned for her to come into the room that she was able to enter. When she did, she fell on the floor under the anointing of the Holy Spirit. Then the gentleman came up and the same occurrence happened to him.

God started showing me certain people in the spirit. My husband and the gentleman went and picked these people up until our bedroom was filled. This happened for approximately four straight hours! The people God showed me in the Spirit were captured and arrested by the anointing of God just as our houseguests were.

All I can say is that the glory of God had filled my room because of the focus on the Blood of Jesus.

Inserts from "Life in the Blood" by Apostle Juanita Ford

Chapter One
Acceptance through the Blood

⚜ *I AM SO GLAD* ⚜ you are reading this book. You are about to experience natural and supernatural changes in your life in Jesus' name.

If you have a copy of my first book "LIFE IN THE BLOOD", you know what was related. If you don't have a copy of the book, here are some subjects discussed:

- The miracle in the New Beginning
- Recognizing the Devil's Attack
- The Source of Life
- Transformed by the Blood
- Fighting the Good Fight
- A New Way of Life
- Testimonies of how people overcame situations through the blood of the Lamb
- How I was raised from the death bed through the pleading of the Blood.

In "LIFE IN THE BLOOD" we show how there is life in the blood of Jesus. When applying the blood to my situation, especially at a time when I was in the hospital, a lady came and applied the blood of Jesus over me. I was close to death, but through the proclaiming of the blood of Jesus, I am alive today.

In this book, we will see how to have victory, through the blood of the Lamb in every area of life. When the Blood of Jesus is applied and meditated on, we will receive victory.

Revelation 12:11 says: and they overcame him (Satan) by the blood of the Lamb and by the word of their testimony; and they loved not their lives unto the death.
You will also read testimonies in the Word of God and about people who took communion for 7, 10, 21, and 30 days or for life. After following these instructions something miraculous will happen.

My husband and I have made a quality and lifetime decision to honor the blood and we are getting results daily. Sometimes people may feel or think that taking communion every day doesn't make a difference. Let me challenge you to honor the Lord and take communion for 10 days over a situation and watch what God does in your life.

My husband and I took communion over our daughter who lives in Delaware over different situations and she would do the same and she would come out victoriously. When I came to the revelation of the importance of taking communion, I shared it with my family and certain members didn't understand it. It wasn't until they received revelatory knowledge and started honoring communion that they saw results and they haven't stopped taking it since. I really needed peace on my job and the Lord asked me if I had taken communion over it. The next day I took what I call a communion "pre-pack" to work and the chaos in leadership changed and peace abided. Once you get a result in one area, you will get results in all areas.
Here is a brief testimony about how I was delivered from the spirit of anger I had towards my husband. When my husband would make me angry, I would internalize the anger. Later,

when I was ready to talk about it again, the situation would explode. While studying about the blood, I was instructed by the Holy Spirit to take communion for 30 days over my anger issues; not that it takes 30 days. That's just what I needed to do. Jesus instituted the Lord's Supper the same night that Judas betrayed Him. He didn't let the betrayal stop Him. He lifted up the bread and cup over the spirit of betrayal and went on about His Father's business. I do the same thing no matter what, and you can too. So I lifted up the bread and cup over the spirit of anger and was delivered in Jesus' name.

John the Baptist proclaims in Saint John 1:29: The next day John seeth Jesus coming unto him, and saith, Behold the Lamb of God, which take away the sin of the world. I recognized that the Blood of the Lamb will take anger away.

Now according to the Bible the only anger we should have is at sin; but, the Word advises not to let the sun go down upon your wrath giving place to the devil (Ephesians 4:25-32).
What do I do when something happens? I go to the blood of the Lamb and the Word of God to see what God the Father has to say about it.

Let's explore how you can receive victory by accepting the blood. The word "acceptance" means: the act of accepting or state of being accepted or approval.
Some people seek acceptance through a certain church, gang, club, family, school, bank, or society. There is nothing wrong with that except when it doesn't stay in the right perspective.
Ephesians 1:6 says to the praise of the glory of His grace, wherein He hath made us accepted in the Beloved.

The blood of the Lamb has made us accepted in the beloved Jesus Christ. Therefore we are to be to the praise of His glory and not our own, for we are bought with the price of the precious blood of Jesus. We know that His blood was not cheap blood but is precious blood that was shed for the whole world. Since we have been accepted through the blood of the Lamb, what are we bringing into the presence of the Heavenly Father? Some people bring different issues into God's presence or before giving thanksgiving, adoration and praise. For example, some bring complaining, crying, fears, doubts, false humility, pride, unforgiveness, spouses, children, jobs, and money, etc. Some of these things are not worth bringing into the presence of the Father; especially, when it's done in with the wrong intention.

Granted some people do not know about bringing the blood or the communion cup of blessings with the bread of the body of Christ into the presence of the Lord; therefore, the Holy Spirit led me to write this book on this subject. There are others who have written books on the cup of blessings and the bread of the body of Christ.

In my own personal life I used to take some of the same things into the presence of my quiet time with the Lord until I learned about honoring the cup of blessings. Communion, first in Hebrews 9:7 says, But into the second went the high priest alone once every year, not without blood, which he offered for himself, and for the errors of the people:

Once in South Carolina I was on my knees praying and crying to the Lord about our finances and the Lord said to me that I might as well get up because He was not moved by my crying. So I got up in obedience and went about my way and the finances that I was crying about turned out all right in Jesus name.

Let's examine the scriptures of Abel and Cain how Abel was accepted through the blood sacrifice and Cain wasn't because he didn't bring what was required into the presence of the Lord.

 Genesis 4:1-7: Adam knew Eve his wife: and she conceived, and bare Cain, and said I, have gotten a man from the Lord.

Adam and Eve came together in a relationship and Eve conceived (received the seed that Adam released) and Cain came into existence. Then Eve made a proclamation saying, "I have gotten a man from the Lord. "It was not from evolution, but from the Lord. Praise the Lord. She spoke a blessing over Cain's life.

[2] And she again bares his brother Abel. And Abel was a keeper of sheep, but Cain was a tiller of the ground.

Adam and Eve once again came together and Eve received Abel who was a keeper of Sheep. Here, the Bible identifies both Abel and Cain's gifting (or occupation): Abel was the keeper of the blood because sheep have blood in them, which is what God looks for. However, Cain watched over something that was already cursed: the ground!

[3] And in process of time it came to pass, that Cain brought of the fruit of the ground an offering unto the Lord.

In the right time Cain brought the Lord an offering. But was the offering acceptable to the Lord? No.

Remember, we cannot just bring anything into the Lord's presence and think that He should accept it. Like Cain, people get rejected for what they bring into the presence of God.

It's like scanning a bank card in a store, for example. Sometimes the scanner will reject the card number because of error on the consumer or the card could be damaged. The blood of the Lamb of God, the Word of God, faith, giving of thanks, rejoicing, forgiveness, the name of Jesus, etc. are right codes that have been applied to get God's attention.

This also reminds me of a husband and wife relationship. The husband wants his wife to come into his presence with thanksgiving in order to get what she wants.

Leviticus 4:5-7: And the priest that is anointed shall take of the bullock's blood, and bring it to the tabernacle of the congregation: And the priest shall dip his finger in the blood, and sprinkle of the blood seven times before the Lord, before the veil of the sanctuary. And the priest shall put some of the blood upon the horns of the altar of sweet incense before the Lord, which is in the tabernacle of the congregation; and shall pour all the blood of the bullock at the bottom of the altar of the burnt offering, which is at the door of the tabernacle of the congregation.

The scripture illustrates the process of the high priest and the blood. The high priest entered the tabernacle with the blood seven times. The number seven means completion. I challenge you to take communion for seven days over any issue. Once you get the victory by taking the Blood, it will become a lifestyle and you will be blessed!

The blood is a tool that will cause us to be accepted into the Father's presence. We cannot go in any kind of way and expect approval or answers.

Remember the Word of God says in Hebrews 9:7, But into the second went the high priest alone once every year, not without blood, which he offered for himself, and for the errors of the people.

There are three things the high priest did when entering into God's presence:

1. He brought the blood
2. He offered the blood for himself, plus
3. He offered the blood for the errors of the people.

Let's continue with Cain and Abel. And Abel, he also brought of the firstlings of his flock and of the fat thereof. And the Lord had respect unto Abel and to his offering: (Genesis 4:4).

There are seven important things that happened in Abel's life when he presented his offering:

1. Abel brought to the Lord the blood first (the firstlings of his flock).
2. Abel presented the first part (his tithe) of his occupation.
3. Abel presented a fat offering (a fat offering and not a little one).
4. Abel received man's highest honor, the Lord's respect.
5. Abel received respect because of the offering he brought. He didn't send his offering by someone else.
6. Abel spent exclusive time with the Lord.
7. Abel didn't depend on people to bring him into the presence of God.
    [5] But unto Cain and to his offering he had not respect. And Cain was very wroth, and his countenance fell.

Why wasn't Cain offering accepted? If we find out what something is not, then we can find out what something is. Six things kept Cain from being accepted:

1. He presented something that was already a curse.
2. Cain didn't bring the blood sacrifice into the presence of the Lord.
3. Cain wasn't respected.
4. Cain brought wrath into the presence of the Lord.
5. Cain had a fallen countenance (face).
6. Cain didn't bring what God asked him to bring.

When Nehemiah was servicing the king and he came into his presence, the king immediately noticed that Nehemiah's face was not joyful. In those days people would not go into the king's presence any kind of way. The same is true with us. We should enter into God's presence giving Him thanks and praising His name.

⁶ And the Lord said unto Cain, Why art thou wroth? And why is thy countenance fallen?

The Lord wanted to know why Cain was angry and why his face was sad.

Sounds like an attitude situation to me. But God knew how to straighten Cain's attitude out. God told Cain that all he had to do was do well by bringing the blood into His presence.

The same is true with us. In order to be accepted by God, we have to do well by giving Him what He wants when we come to Him.

I Samuel 2:30 says, "...for them that honor me I will honor, and they that despise me shall be lightly esteemed." Honor the blood and the blood will honor you. Make light of the blood and the blood will make light of you.

⁷ If thou doest well, shalt thou not be accepted? And if thou doest not well, sin lieth at the door. And unto thee shall be his desire, and thou shalt rule over him.

A choice was given to Cain to make a change and he did.

Here is a testimony by a young lady from Jonesboro, Georgia, who decided to make a change in her life by honoring communion for 30 days. The Jonesboro woman says, "While taking communion for 30 days, I read Matthew 15:21-28. Even though I had read the scriptures and heard them preached from the pulpit many times, they had never come to life to me before as they had now. The most significant part of the scripture was verse 27. I could not get pass the crumbs; each time I broke the bread during the communion, I was always curious about the crumbs. They were a part of the bread and they still had the same meaning as the whole bread. But what about the crumbs, I kept asking myself. One day God answered my question. He revealed the reason the Canaanite woman said that even the dogs eat the crumbs from the masters' table. It was because Jesus was sent to restore Israel back to God first, and she wanted part of what He had then.

God showed me that I had always expected crumbs for myself, and that I belonged to Him. I could have the whole loaf, and not just the fallen table crumbs, because God is able." Tanger H. – Jonesboro, GA.

We see in this testimony how she receives revelation from honoring communion. Praise the Lord!

Chapter Two
Victory through a Test

⌘

Remember open-book tests in school? The exams that teachers sometimes gave to students that allowed them to use the particular book to assist them during an exam. The teacher would assign certain chapters one day and exam students the next based on their assigned reading. The answers to open-book tests are always easy to find if a student properly read and highlighted certain parts of the reading.

The same applies to believers. When we are going through a test we must read the Bible and meditate on the Word so that we can continually overcome the devil's trials.

Let's see how to get victory when we go through a test by examining the life of Noah.

Genesis 8:20-22 says
[20]And Noah built an altar unto the Lord, and took of every clean beast and of every clean fowl, and offered burnt offering on the altar:[21] And the Lord smelled a sweet savor; and the Lord said in his heart, I will not again curse the ground any more for man's sake: for the imagination of man's heart is evil from his youth; neither will I again smite any more everything living as I have done.[22] While the earth remaineth, seedtime and harvest, and cold and heat, and summer and winter, and day and night shall not cease.

Noah received victory when he built God an altar after spending 40 days and nights (the time of testing) in the ark. Though Noah was in the ark for a long time, he came out victorious.

The scriptures show what Noah's focus was after he came out of the ark with his family. Noah didn't focus on the natural: food, shopping, having a party, etc.; he focused on the supernatural: a blood sacrifice to worship God for keeping him, his family, and the animals through the time of testing. When others were destroyed, he and his family were kept safe. This is something to give God thanks for.

When Noah offered up the blood sacrifice, the scriptures say that the Lord "smelled a sweet savor." When the blood is brought to God it makes things smell sweet instead of stinking. Sin stinks in the nostrils of God. When Jesus died on the cross with the sins of the world upon Him, He said, "... My God, my God, why hast thou forsaken me" (Mark 15:34[b])? Jesus felt forsaken because His father God turned away from the sin laid to his son's charge. The honoring of the blood turns God the Father back to us. I am reminded of how Isaiah talks about sin being like "scarlet and crimson" (Isaiah 1:18). Both are very dark in color but the blood makes them "white as snow."

An old familiar song says, "What can wash away my sins? Nothing but the blood of Jesus. What can make me whole again? Nothing but the blood of Jesus.

Noah's blood sacrifice caused God to make a promise of not cursing the ground or smiting every living thing as He had done before. So the blood exchanged the curse for the covenant rainbow promise which we often see in the sky today.

Once I was working on a job and I asked the Lord if I was there for a trial? The Lord asked me if I had taken communion over the situation and I said no. The next day I honored communion at my work locker and that same day the situation changed. I left in peace. Even the person who I had challenges with ended up celebrating me, when I left that job.

Another time I was victorious through the blood was over the ministry my husband and I had in College Park, Georgia in 2002.We needed to hear from God about the next step in our ministry. After honoring the blood, the Lord told us to release our entire congregation because we had trained them from newborn babes in Christ to mature ministers. The answer came and we praised the Lord!

Chapter Three
Spoken Words Sealed With the Blood

When we speak God's word, we are speaking what God the Father has spoken over our lives and it will come to pass as we give God's Word back to Him.

Abram received words spoken to him by God and then God sealed those words through a sacrifice. He spoke with the blood when an altar was built to Him. In those days when an altar was built, a blood sacrifice was placed on the altar. How can we build an altar in our lives or houses to the Lord today? We can build an altar by honoring the communion cup and the Word of God on a daily basis.

Genesis 12:7 And the Lord appeared unto Abram, and said, unto thy seed will I give this land: and there builded he an altar unto the Lord, who appeared unto him.

The Lord gave Abram a Word (a promise) that his seed would receive the land where the Ca-an-an-ite (the world system) dwelled. Abram sealed the word of the Lord with a blood sacrifice by building an altar unto the Lord who appeared unto him. When the Lord speaks a word to us, we need to write the word and seal it with the blood just like Abram did by offering up the communion cup to the Father.

God made Abram a promise that he would give his seed the land where they dwelt. We are the seed of Abraham through

Jesus Christ and there are lands and territories that are promised to us that we must take by force in Jesus Name!

Genesis 12:8-9 and he removed from thence unto a mountain on the east of Beth-el, and pitched his tent, having Beth-el on the west, and Hai on the east: and there he builded an altar unto the Lord, and called upon the name of the Lord. Abram journeyed, going on still toward the south.

After Abram received the Word of the Lord, he went to the land of Beth-el and Hai and built another altar to the Lord to establish taking the land over. The blood established the Word of God and gave the land to Abram. He received the victory through the Word spoken to him to possess the land.

In the early 90s, my husband and I believed God for a new house. We wanted a house that no one had ever lived in, and we got it. We had so much favor that when we closed on the house, the lenders gave us money. We really possessed the land!

Chapter Four
Victory through the Blood Over Strife

Webster's Illustrated Contemporary Dictionary defines strife as "angry contention; fighting; any contest; the act of striving, strenuous endeavor against another person."

In Genesis 13:1-9 we will see how Abram gained victory over strife through the blood. When Abram built an altar to God in Genesis 12, it prevented him from unwise situations.

And Abram went up out of Egypt, he, and his wife, and all that he had, and Lot with him, into the south. And Abram was very rich in cattle, in silver, and in gold. And he went on his journeys from the south even to Beth-el, unto the place where his tent had been at the beginning, between Beth-el and Hai; unto the place of the altar, which he had made there at the first: and there Abram called on the name of the Lord. And Lot also, which went with Abram, had flocks, and herds, and tents. And the land was not able to bear them, that they might dwell together: for their substance was great, so that they could not dwell together. There was strife between the herdsmen of Abram's cattle and the herdsmen of Lot's cattle: and the Canaanite and the Perizzite dwelled then in the land. And Abram said unto Lot Let there be no strife, I pray thee, between me and thee, and between my herdsmen and thy herdsman; for we be brethren. Is not the whole land before thee? Separate thyself. I pray thee, from me; if thou will take the left hand, then I will go

15

to the right; or if thou depart to the right hand, then I will go to the left.

When Abram built the altar to the Lord the first time something was established. He went back to the place a second time to offer up another blood sacrifice. We have the liberty to bring the blood covenant before the Lord as many times as we need to and He will always bring about a change.

The scriptures say let everything be established in the mouth of two or three witnesses.

II Corinthians 13:1 says, this is the third time I am coming to you. In the mouth of two or three witnesses shall every word be established?

Matthew 18:16 says, But if he will not hear thee, then take with thee one or two more, that in the mouth of two or three witnesses every word may be established.

The key point is this: there must be something established in every situation; then, the Word and the blood will do it.

Let's return to Abram. Genesis 13:14-18:

And the Lord said unto Abram, after that Lot was separated from him, Lift up now thine eyes, and look from the place where thou art northward, and southward, and eastward, and westward;[15] For all the land which thou seest, to thee will I give it, and to thy seed forever.16 And I will make thy seed as the dust of the earth: so that if a man can number the dust of the earth, then shall thy seed also be numbered. [17]Arise, walk through the land in the length of it and in the breadth of it; for I will give it unto thee. [18] Then Abram removed his tent, and came and dwelt in the plain of Mamre, which is in Hebron, and built there an altar unto the Lord.

When Abram established the blood (the altar), strife was driven out of his household and his ministry. The blood gave Abram victory over strife even with his family members. The communion cup will give us victory over strife.

Allow me to be transparent. When my husband and I pastored our first church in the early 90s, I dealt with strife and anger. We didn't agree on certain things in the ministry and as a result, we brought those issues into our home. I decided one day that enough was enough. I realized that strife was not the will of God for our marriage or ministry. I honored the communion for peace in our home continuously and prayed Ephesians 1:15-23 that our eyes would be opened to what God wanted in our lives and the blood worked; Victory through the Blood!

Chapter Five
Victory to Have God as Source

❧❦❧

And the King of Sodom went out to meet him after his return from the slaughter of Chedorlaomer, and of the kings that were with him, at the valley of Shaveh, which is the king's dale. And Melchizedek king of Salem brought forth bread and wine: and he was the priest of the most High God. And he blessed him, and said, Blessed be Abram of the most High God, possessor of heaven and earth: And blessed be the most High God, which hath delivered thine enemies into thy hand. And he gave him tithes of all. And the king of Sodom said unto Abram, Give me the persons, and take the goods to thyself. And Abram said to the king of Sodom, I have lift up mine hand unto the Lord, the most High God, the possessor of heaven and earth, That I will not take from a thread even to a shoelatchet, and that I will not take any thing that is thine, lest thou shouldest say, I have made Abram rich: Save only that which the young men have eaten, and the portion of the men which went with me, Aner, Eschol, and Mamre; let them take their portion.
-Genesis 14: 17-24

The king of Sodom met Abram after he returned back a victorious slaughter of Chedorlaomer and the other kings with him.

Verse 18 says that Melchizedek, king of Salem and servant of the most High God, brought bread and wine which symbolize Jesus the Lamb, also known as the Bread of Life, coming to the earth and slain from the foundation of the world. He is the High Priest of the Living God.

Verse 19 & 20 Melchizedek king of Salem took the bread and wine and began to speak the blessings over Abram:

1.   Blessed be Abram of the Most High God, possessor of heaven and earth.
2.   Blessed be the Most High God which hath delivered thine enemies into thy hand.

This is a great example proving that we should take communion over our enemies. Call them out by name, bless them according to the Word of God, and take note of the results (Matthew 5:43-45).

After Melchizedek spoke blessings over Abram, tithes were given.

Because bread and wine were present, Abram's eyes were opened to see that he needed to keep God and not man as his source. The use of the word "man" will be a chance for blessings to flow through.

Luke 24:30-32 speaks of how Jesus sat at meat with the two on the Emmaus road. When Jesus blessed the bread and gave to them, their eyes were opened because the bread and wine were there. The scripture also mentions how their hearts burned along the way as Jesus expounded on the scriptures. Their hearts burned because the Lamb that was slain (the Blood) ministered to them. The blood cleans the heart of sins.

When we take communion over our sins, the blood will clean our heart also. The blood of Jesus the Lamb releases the blessings upon our lives when we speak what the Word of God says about us.

1. All these blessings shall come upon us and overtake us as we hearken unto the word of the Lord our God to observe and to do his commandments. V. 1, 2
2. We shall be blessed in the city and in the field. V. 3
3. We shall be blessed in the fruit of our body (health). V.3
4. We shall be blessed in the fruit of our ground. V. 3
5. We shall be blessed with Goodly things V. 3
6. We shall be blessed with basket and store. V. 5
7. We shall be blessed when we come in. V. 6
8. We shall be blessed when we go out. V. 6
9. We shall see our enemies smitten before our face seven ways. V.7
10. The Lord shall command the blessing upon us in our storehouses. V.8
11. The Lord shall command the blessing in all that we set our hand to. V. 8
12. The Lord shall bless us in the land we are in. V. 8
13. The Lord shall establish us a holy people unto Himself. V. 9
14. The Lord shall empower us to walk in His ways. V. 9
15. All people shall see that we are called by the name of the Lord and be afraid of us. V. 10
16. The Lord shall make us plenteous in goods. V. 11
17. The Lord shall bless us in the fruit of our body (mentioned twice to get your attention from God). V. 11
18. The Lord shall bless us in the fruit of our ground. V. 11
19. The Lord shall bless us with land. V. 11
20. The Lord shall open unto us his good treasure. V.12
21. The Lord shall open the heaven to give us rain into the land in his season. V.12

22. The Lord shall bless all the work of our hands. V. 12
23. The Lord said we shall lend unto many nations. V. 12
24. The Lord said we shall not borrow but lend (we can be the bank for others). V. 12
25. The Lord made us the head. V. 13
26. The Lord shall cause us not to be the tail. V. 13
27. We shall be above only. V. 13
28. We shall not be beneath. V. 13
29. We shall not go aside from these words (blessings) to the right or to the left! V. 14
30. We shall not go after other gods to serve them to receive the blessings. V.14

These are 30 blessings listed above from Deuteronomy 28:1-14. What if we prayed one blessing daily with communion? Imagine what would happen to our lives if we release our faith to each promise?

Martha's story:
I had a blessed time fellowshipping with the Lord during my 30 days of communion. As my roommate Tanger and I prepared to honor the communion, we prayed, asked for forgiveness, and read I Corinthians 11:23-26. Our time of communion seemed to lead to a time of intense intercession. If we petitioned the Lord for anything, He seemed to answer during our time of communion.

One insight I learned while honoring communion was that on the night that the Lord had communion He blessed the bread, broke it, and gave to his disciples. I believe if we bless the Lord, give ourselves completely –withholding nothing– and allow Him to break us; then, and only then will we be ready to be given that others may eat of our fruit (our good works). We will be a blessing to others and be the instrument that the Lord uses to break things off of them, so they in turn may be given.

While in the silence, God allowed me to receive another revelation while honoring communion. I've found that the closer I come into God's presence, the quieter I become. Silence is good. It allows God to minister to my heart without having to fight through my emotions. Silence speaks volumes. I hear more in the silence because there's nothing or no one else fighting for my attention. For me, being in the silence is like snuggling up with a loved one and the contentment of just being in their presence where no words are needed.

This chapter shows us that there is victory in knowing that the Lord is our source; He is our Shepherd and we shall not want.

Chapter Six
Victory through the Blood to inherit Land

The scriptures show us that God would promise the children of Israel and the body of Christ what they can possess through a blood sacrifice. In Genesis 15:7-10, Abram received his inherited land through a blood sacrifice to the Lord.

Galatians 3:29 calls believers the "seed of Abraham" through Christ Jesus. There's a familiar song called "The Blessing of Abraham." One line in particular that rings or echo in my spirit is "Get your inheritance!" God wants us to get our inheritance. The whole point of the children of Israel coming out of Egypt was for them to possess the land that flows with milk and honey. There's something about ownership verses paying monthly rent. Ownership to me means possessing something that is exclusively mine. It belongs to me.

In Webster's Contemporary Dictionary, the word "inherits" means 1. to receive as property or a title, by succession or will; 2. to receive (traits, qualities, etc.) by or as if by heredity; and 3. to come into or possess an inheritance.

So we understand that Abraham's promise from God was that He would bless Abram and his descendants.

Abram obeyed God when he left his kindred, father's house and country. The result of his obedience was when he inherited the land God promised. Likewise, when we obey God's voice, He will give us the land to inherit.

Later, Abram asked God for confirmation on how he would inherit the land. God specifically instructed Abram to sacrifice a three-year-old heifer, female goat and ram and also a turtledove and a young pigeon. In other words, God wanted a blood sacrifice and Abram was obedient. When he sacrificed the animals God instructed, God spoke to him about what was going to happen with his seed. God said they would be strangers in a land that was not theirs and shall serve God; even when God judged, He would cause Abram's seed to come out with great substance.

The same is true with the body of Christ. We've been serving in this world system for years, yet God sent Jesus Christ, the blood sacrifice, as payment for our spiritual and physical inheritance. Some may ask the same question as Abram: "How shall I know that I inherit the land?" or "Will it happen as I believe God?" Get alone with God the Father and offer up to Him the BLOOD (communion) along with the promises in His Word and get an answer.

My husband and I lost some land in the past, but we know that God will restore everything the devil stole from us. We know that more will come through the blood of the Lamb and the word of our testimonies. We will get back all that was stolen and more. I'm reminded of what David proclaimed, "I shall recover all." We shall recover all our land and more in Jesus name!

After Abram presented the blood sacrifice, God told him the names of the land that He will give to Abram's seed.

And it came to pass, that when the sun went down and it was dark, behold a smoking furnace, and a burning lamp that passed between those pieces. In the same day the Lord made a covenant with Abram saying unto thy seed have I given this land from the river Egypt unto the great river, the Euphrates: The Kenites, and the Kenizzites, and the Kadmonites, And the Hittites, and the Perizzites, and the Rephaims, And the Amorites, and the Canaanites, and the Girgashites, and the Jebusites (Genesis 15:17-21).

We are the seed of Abraham through Jesus Christ and the Body of Christ, and we shall get our inheritance.

Praise the Lord!

God gave Abraham 12 names of land that his seed would inherit. Jesus also had 12 Apostles who He gave authority to possess their territory. My husband and I will live in a house bigger and better than the houses we lost in the past, praise the Lord. GO INHERIT THE LAND!

Chapter Seven
Covenant of Victory in the BLOOD

What is a covenant? Webster's Illustrated Contemporary Dictionary (Encyclopedic Edition), defines "covenant" as a formal and binding agreement entered into by two or more persons or parties; a compact. It is also God's promises to mankind as set forth in the Bible.

For example, David and Jonathan made a covenant with each other in I Samuel 18: 1-4. Jonathan loved David as his own soul. He made an exchange with David by giving him his own robe, garments, sword, bow, and girdle. There was nothing that could separate Jonathan and David from each other; not even Jonathan's natural father. Once I accepted Jesus Christ as my Lord and Savior, I became like Paul that wrote in Romans 8: 35 - 39 ...Nothing can separate me from the love of God the Father. Nor height, not depth, nor any other creature, shall be able to separate us from the love of God, which is in Christ Jesus our Lord. That awesome love covenant only came through the blood of the Lamb.

And when Abram was ninety years old and nine, the Lord appeared to Abram, and said unto him, I am the Almighty God; walk before me, and be thou perfect. And I will make my covenant between me and thee, and will multiply thee exceedingly (Genesis 17:1, 2).

At the age of 99 the Lord appeared to Abram and reminded him that He is the Almighty God. His walk before God was so perfect (mature), that God made a covenant with him to multiply him exceedingly.

Genesis 17:3 - 5 ³And Abram fell on his face: and God talked with him, saying, ⁴As for me, behold, my covenant is with thee, and thou shalt be a father of many nations.
After God spoke to Abram about the covenant, he fell on his face and worshipped God for the covenant he established. ⁵Neither shall thy name any more be called Abram, but thy name shall be called Abraham; for a father of many nations have I made thee.

Abram's name change is a pivotal point in scripture. Through a covenant a person's name can be changed, which is what God did to Abram. He changed his name from Abram to Abraham: the father of many nations.

When a woman gets married, for example, her last name should change from her maiden name to her new married name because a marriage covenant has been established. She no longer possesses her father's name, but her new covenant name. When we accepted Jesus Christ as our Lord and Savior, our name changed from "sinner" to "saint." Our changed covenant name puts us in another position where we are seated with Christ in heavenly places.
Genesis 17:6 And I will make thee exceeding fruitful, and I will make nations of thee, and kings shall come out of thee.
God promised Abraham three things:
      1. To make him exceedingly fruitful
      2. To make nations from him and
      3. To make kings come from him.

Ephesians 3:20 says Now unto Him that is able to do exceeding abundantly above all that we ask or think according to the power that worketh in us." Let's take a look at some exceeding abundant promises found in Ephesians 3:16-19:

1. We are strengthened with might by his spirit in the inner man.
2. Christ dwells in our hearts by faith.
3. We are rooted and grounded in love.
4. We are able to comprehend with all saints God's breadth, length, depth, and height.
5. We know the love of Christ which passeth knowledge.
6. We are filled with all the fullness of God.

Genesis 17:7-14 And I will establish my covenant between me and thee and thy seed after thee in their generations for an everlasting covenant, to be a God unto thee, and to thy seed after thee. And I will give unto thee and to thy seed after thee, the land wherein thou art a stranger, all the land of Canaan, for an everlasting possession; and I will be their God. And God said unto Abraham, Thou shalt keep my covenant therefore, thou, and thy seed after thee in their generations. This is my covenant, which ye shall keep, between me and you and thy seed after thee; every man child among you shall be circumcised. And ye shall circumcise the flesh of your foreskin; and it shall be a token of the covenant betwixt me and you. And he that is eight days old shall be circumcised among you, every man child in your generations, he that is born in the house, or bought with money of any stranger, which is not of thy seed. He that is born in thy house, and he that is bought with thy money, must needs be circumcised: and my covenant shall be in your flesh for an everlasting covenant. And the uncircumcised man child whose flesh of his foreskin is not circumcised, that soul shall be cut off from his people; he hath broken my covenant.

Let's expound on this passage. In verse 7 God established His everlasting covenant with Abraham and his descendants to be a God to them all. We the believers are the "seed after him" as the scriptures say; meaning that, we are in Abraham's lineage through Jesus Christ's shed blood.

In verse 8 God again made a covenant with Abraham that He would give to him and his seed after him the land for an everlasting possession and be their God. In verse 9 God commands Abraham and his family to keep the covenant that He would establish with him.

Verse 10 introduces the instructions God gave Abraham in order to receive the covenant promise. God told Abraham that he and every male child shall be circumcised (cut).

Verse 11 explains how the circumcision, the cutting of the flesh's foreskin and the shedding of blood, is a token (sign) of the covenant between God and Abraham. Hebrews 9:22 says, "And almost all things are by the law purged with blood; and without shedding of blood is no remission." Circumstances in life change by the shedding of blood along with the Word of God.

In verse 12 God instructed that the circumcision should be done to 8-day old males bought with money of any stranger (slaves) who was not of Abraham's seed.

Verse 13 illustrates how the covenant in the flesh (natural) brought about an everlasting spiritual covenant. When Jesus shed His blood in the natural, an everlasting covenant with God the Father was made in the spirit for us. Verse 14 introduces God's warning that any male child that was uncircumcised would be cut off from the everlasting covenant with God the Father.

Through God's instructed blood covenant Abraham was always victorious. Every time someone was born in his house and circumcised, Abraham reminded God of the promise He made to Abraham and his seed. The same is true with The Lord's Supper (communion): every time we honor the Lord's communion, we are establishing and reestablishing the everlasting covenant with Him.

Verses 15-27 tells Abraham's response when God instructed him to honor the blood covenant. God also changed Sari's name to Sarah, the mother of many nations, because of Abraham's obedience to God's instruction. As a result of his and Sarah's obedience, God promised them something better: a son born out of their own bowels despite their old age. Whenever we make a covenant with God something better always happens.

In Genesis 21:4 God promised Abraham and Sarah a son and Abraham carried out the instructions God gave about circumcision on the eight day. Since we have accepted Jesus Christ as Lord, we must continue to honor the covenant He made with us by honoring the blood of the Lamb (communion). In the next chapter we'll break down Abraham's test of obedience by the promise from God and discuss how provisions can be made by honoring the Blood.

Chapter Eight
Victory through the Blood for Provision

And it came to pass after these things that God did tempt Abraham, and said unto him, Abraham: and he said, Behold, here I am. ² And he said, Take now thy son, thine only son Isaac, whom thou lovest, and get thee into the land of Moriah; and offer him there for a burnt offering upon one of the mountains which I will tell thee of. ³ And Abraham rose up early in the morning, and saddled his ass, and took two of his young men with him, and Isaac his son, and clave the wood for the burnt offering, and rose up, and went unto the place of which God had told him. -Genesis 22:1-3

When we are looking for God's provision, we must go to the place where He hath told us to go and offer unto Him a blood sacrifice through the communion cup. There He will give us clarity about the assignment He has for our lives.

Genesis 22:9 says, "And they came to the place which God had told him of; and Abraham built an altar there, and laid the wood in order, and bound Isaac his son, and laid him on the altar upon the wood."

Provision was made when Abraham obeyed God, believed God, and built an altar.

Genesis 22: 13-14: And Abraham lifted up his eyes, and looked, and behold behind him a ram caught in a thicket by his horns: and Abraham went and took the ram, and offered him up for a burnt offering in the stead of his son. 14 And Abraham called the name of that place Jehovah-jireh; as it is said to this day, in the mount of the Lord it shall be seen.

These verses show how God provided every need for Abraham and he proclaimed God as his Jehovah-jireh, "the Lord's provision shall be seen." Abraham's victory for his provision only came when he offered up a blood sacrifice unto the Lord. Here are two testimonies about how God provided for his people when they honored the communion. During the summer of 2005, Pastor Deborah Braxton attended a women's conference in Atlanta, Georgia. Back home in Maryland, her home phone services were terminated due to a large debt. Pastor Braxton understood the value of taking communion, and by the time she returned home, her home phone services were restored. How does that happen, you may ask? By honoring the Blood of the Lamb, Hallelujah!

All things matter to God the Father whether small or large. When we acknowledge Him in all our ways, He makes a way for more favor to occur in our lives. In March 2004, Dana Lewis had been experiencing EXTREME FAVOR in different places. She wanted her car to get detailed and was able to get it done for free! These women of God saw God's provisional work in the smallest areas of their lives, and it happened at the right time by honoring the communion cup.

Here is my testimony about God's provision in my life through honoring the communion cup. In 2007 my husband and I wrote down all our creditors on a piece of paper. From the smallest to the largest, the debt totaled $5,134.49. The only income we had was his military retirement check, some speaking engagements, profit from my book <u>LIFE IN THE BLOOD</u> before it went to

Author House at that time. We began to thank God the Father every day for more speaking engagements, the spirit of wealth, money to pay the creditors, and more strategies to sell and publish books to nations. Through the law of diligence every creditor was paid in full before the end of 2007! We praise God the Father in Jesus name!

During the week of July 4, 2007, my husband and I needed a brand new car. We went to the Lexus and Ford dealership. At that time we didn't drive either car off the lot, but we kept the vision alive. We took communion and by faith believed that God would provide for us to do His assignment in the earth. We went to the Toyota dealer and the provision was there. We could have even purchased two cars for the price of one. We had come out of bankruptcy because God is bigger than a bankruptcy.

Chapter Nine
Victory in the Blood for Answers

And God said unto Jacob, Arise, go up to Beth-el, and dwell there: and make there an altar unto God that appeared unto thee when thou fleddest from the face of Esau thy brother. [2]Then Jacob said unto his household, and to all that were with him, Put away the strange gods that are among you, and be clean, and change your garments: [3]And let us arise, and go up to Beth-el; and I will make there an altar unto God, who answered me in the day of my distress, and was with me in the way which I went. – Genesis 35:1-3

God reminded Jacob to arise (change his position) and go up to Bethel, stay there and make an altar (blood sacrifice) unto God. When he made the altar, God appeared to him. When Jacob ran from his brother Esau, after stealing his birthright, God still protected him because of the blood. When God told Jacob to build an altar, he immediately obeyed.

In verses 2 & 3, Jacob commanded his household to put away strange gods, to be clean and to change their garments, because they were going into the presence of the Lord to offer up a blood sacrifice. They could not bring things that would displease God, if they wanted a victorious answer. Jacob knew that when he built an altar, or offered up the blood, he would receive an answer for his life because the blood is life.

God protected Jacob from the terror of the cities that were around them. They could not touch Jacob and his family because they had offered the blood upon the altar. VICTORY!

Genesis 35:7: And he built there an altar, and called the place El-beth-el: because there God appeared unto him, when he fled from the face of his brother.

Later, Jacob came to another challenging place in life, built an altar, and called that place El-bethel. At El-bethel God appeared to Jacob and changed his name to Israel. Then God released blessings on his life to be fruitful, to multiply, and to be a nation and a company of nations. God also said that kings shall come from his loins, and the land that God gave Abraham and Isaac would belong to him and his descendants. The victory was won through the blood at the altar for blessings.

In September 2006, Jeanetta Gines and her husband needed a breakthrough in their family, a job for her husband, and a church home. Jeanetta's friend, Vanessa Stanley, introduced her to my first book LIFE IN THE BLOOD. After reading the book twice in one night, Jeanetta shared it with her husband. They read about taking communion and did it for the job and other answers they needed. Within a week's time God blessed her husband with a job, they received direction on a church home; and peace came into their home and lives. Truly there is victory in the blood and the Word of God.

I had a book signing on August 3, 2006 for LIFE IN THE BLOOD at an army base in Atlanta. A lady named Jacqueline purchase my book and when I returned to the base two weeks later, she shared with me that after reading it she had taken communion and had gotten results. God blessed her with a job promotion. And that wasn't all that happened to Jacqueline. Her ex-husband who lived far from her prevented her from seeing her children. After she read my book, she took communion over that situation in particular and God worked it out in her favor!

After taking communion for three days, April received a bonus at work in 2005. What makes this blessing all the more outstanding was that she had only been on the job for three and a half months!

I had seven specific things I believed God for. After a week of taking communion, all seven have come to pass. HALLELUJAH!

Baya testifies that taking communion every day in her home has brought a new level of peace into her home and life. "My relationship with God has become all the more intimate," she says. I am able to hear Him clearer. He speaks to me more than usual and has given me new sight. I have new eyes to recognize the prophetic and apostolic gifting. As I minister the Word of God, He gives me new revelations of His Word, love, new visions and ideas for His body and faith. Taking communion every day brings me closer to the Father God. John 6:56 says, "He that eateth my flesh, and drinketh my blood, dwelleth in me, and I in Him." There's no other place I'd rather be.

When we apply the communion to any area of life for an answer, we will find that the Blood truly works. First, find out what the Word of God says about what you believe God for and offer up the communion cup for an answer. Even when you are at a crossroad in life, take the Blood and you will find that the BLOOD WORKS!

Chapter Ten
Victory through the Blood over Enemies

What is an enemy? An enemy is one who hates or bears ill will toward another; a foe. It is one who is hostile to an organization, idea, nation, or military force.

How do we get victory over our enemies? First, we must do it according to the Word of God.

Matthew 5:43-45:Ye have heard that it hath been said, Thou shalt love thy neighbor, and hate thine enemy. [44]But I say unto you, Love your enemies, bless them that curse you, do good to them that hate you, and pray for them which despitefully use you, and persecute you; [45]That ye may be the children of your Father which is in heaven: for he maketh his sun to rise on the evil and on the good, and sendeth rain on the just and on the unjust.

When doing communion over your enemies practice what the scripture says:

1. Love your enemies.
2. Bless them when they curse you.
3. Do good to them when they hate you.
4. Pray for them when they despitefully use you.
5. Pray for them when they persecute you.
6. Feed them if they are hungry.
7. Give them something to drink if they are thirsty.

After reciting the scripture, you can pray this prayer: "Father, according to your Word, as I am honoring the communion cup I walk in love toward my enemies. I bless them that curse me, I do good to them that hate me, I pray for them who despitefully use me and persecute me. Also, according to Psalm 23:5, You, Father, have prepared a table before me in the presence of mine enemies; You anoint my head with oil and my cup runs over. Psalm 110:1 says, 'The Lord said unto my Lord, Sit thou at my right hand, until I make thine enemies thy footstool.' So I thank You for Your Word coming to pass in my life about my enemies in Jesus' name, and I know the battle is not mine but the Lord's." In Genesis 37:31-33, here we encounter Joseph's dilemma where his brothers became his enemies.

And they took Joseph's coat, and killed a kid of the goats, and dipped the coat in the blood. And they sent the coat of many colors, and they brought it to their father; and said this have we found: know now whether it be thy son's coat or no. And he knew it, and said, It is my son's coat; an evil beast hath devoured him; Joseph is without doubt rent in pieces.

When Joseph's brothers dipped his coat of many colors into blood, it prepared Joseph for his future reign in Egypt. The blood goes before us and gives us favor. Joseph's coat gave him favor ahead of time before reaching his palace destination. Similarly, the blood of Jesus goes before us to help us reach our "palace destination" or purposed destiny (mansions) that He has prepared for us in Heaven. In the earth, the blood of Jesus Christ will give us the victory over our enemies in Jesus Name.

When the brothers showed the coat of many colors to their father, he immediately recognized it because he had given it to Joseph. The coat of many colors represents the nations from the north, east, west, and south to come under Joseph's protection and have their needs met. Likewise, Jesus' blood was shed to open up and allow all nations to come to God the Father who recognize and accept His Son. God gave the coat (His Son) for the world and shed His blood for all mankind. When we come into the presence of the Heavenly Father with the blood on our lips, lifting up the communion cup, He recognizes us because we are honoring Him through the blood.

Here is how Joseph received the victory over his enemies while in (prison) Genesis 40 and 41.

Genesis 40:1-4 and it came to pass after these things, that the butler of the king of Egypt and his baker had offended their lord the king of Egypt. Something came to pass in the nation of Egypt where his officers offended him.

[2]And Pharaoh was wroth against two of his officers, against the chief of the butlers, and against the chief of the bakers. The offense in verse one made Pharaoh wroth (angry) with two of his chief officers, the butler and baker. There is a consequence when the king is offended, so he sent the butler and baker away.

3And he put them in ward in the house of the captain of the guard, into the prison, the place where Joseph was bound. In verse [3] Pharaoh put the chief of the butler (wine) and the chief of the baker (bread) into prison, the same place where Joseph was bound. Look at God's divine intervention. He directed Pharaoh to put the blood and the bread in the same place Joseph was to illustrate that the blood will restore us and place us above our enemies. The very situation that was meant for bad is the same situation the Lord will turn around and make good. Even though Joseph's brothers sold him into slavery (the bad), God restored Joseph better than before and made him second in command, (The good).

[4]And the captain of the guard charged Joseph with them, and he served them: and they continued a season in ward. When the butler (wine) and the baker (bread) were put into Joseph's charge, Joseph served them.

As the story goes on, the butler and baker both had dreams about Pharaoh doing something to them. They told Joseph the dreams and he interpreted them. The butler's dream was good, and when the baker saw that Joseph gave the butler a good word, he wanted Joseph to interpret his dream. When Joseph gave the baker his word, however, it was not a good word. The word (dream interpretation) that Joseph gave manifested. Joseph said that Pharaoh would hang the baker in three days and he did. When Joseph interpreted the butler's dream, he told him that his position in the palace would be restored by the Pharaoh. Remember the baker represents the bread, Christ's body. In the end, the baker was hung from a tree just as Jesus gave His body for us to be hung from a tree. Likewise, the butler represents wine or Christ's blood. The butler received the word from Joseph about being restored and that is what the blood did; restored him back to his position. The same is true with the blood of Jesus. The blood was shed for us and restored us back to our rightful position in the Garden of Eden before sin came. The blood is a restorer.

The blood will always remember those who honor it. Make much of the blood and the blood will make much of you. Make much out of prayer and prayer will produce much out of you. Remember that we are spirits who have a soul and live in a body. Whatever we feed our spirits will manifest in our lives.

At one time, it seemed like the butler (wine) had forgotten Joseph, but God always remembers the blood covenant that He made with His people. He will cause the blood upon our lives to restore us back. Remember Joseph was in a place of authority before being in prison and the blood restored him back. This time it was better than before. God the Father will restore us better than before. Through Jesus' blood we have been restored back in relationship with the Father and that relationship is better than what Adam and Eve had in the garden. Hebrews 12:24 says,

"And to Jesus the mediator of the new covenant, and to the blood of sprinkling, that speaketh better things than that of Abel."

Later, God caused Pharaoh to have a dream that needed Joseph's interpretation. Through that process God was placing a demand on Joseph's gift, a gift He gave him at birth.
The anointing will find us and bring us before great people, because the Lord has a need of that gift. He put each of our gifts inside us for His kingdom's purpose.
When Joseph interpreted the king's dream and served the butler and baker while in prison, God began the restoration process. The blood restored him because the butler was reminded of how Joseph had interpreted his dream and urged the King to call Joseph to interpret his dream. When we serve the bread and the wine in honor of Jesus' blood that was shed for us, we are restored. Joseph received the victory over his enemies through the blood.
Do you have enemies? Well welcome to the club. Our enemies are really our promotion. Daniel 6:1-28 talks about how Daniel's enemies did not want him to pray to God so they used the very thing he loved against him: his relationship with God. They couldn't stop Daniel from serving God; but, they actually promoted him by being his enemies. Verse 6:28 says that"…Daniel prospered in the reign of Darius and in the reign of Cyrus the Persian."

In my personal life, I have gotten victory over my enemies. When my husband and I needed money to pay our creditors, we took the bread and the wine over them, prayed over them, and the Heavenly Father paid them in full.

41

Even Jesus served His enemy; the one who would betray Him, at the table of The Last Supper. His enemy was revealed; Jesus got the victory; and returned to the Father in a greater way. Cain was his brother Abel's enemy when he took his life; but, Abel's blood still spoke from the ground. Nehemiah had Sanballet and others as enemies; but, the Jews did not stop rebuilding the wall. Their enemies ended up promoting them (Nehemiah 4:1). Noah's enemies probably laughed at him as he built the ark that God told him to build; but, he got the last laugh when all except he and his family were destroyed. David had many enemies; but, he got the victory over them. He often asked God not to let his enemies triumph over him.

2 Kings 3:21-25 says that the sun shined on the water when the Israelites went to fight a battle. The enemies thought they had conquered Israel and started killing themselves. When they got to their camp, they realized they were facing Israel. The blood gave the victory over their enemies and will do the same for us. Even our enemies will promote us.

Testimony: My husband used communion to bring peace to a semi-hostile situation as he dealt with a supervisor and his taste for secular music in the workplace. The supervisor and my husband worked approximately two years for the same company. Each had their own way about themselves and knew each other's convictions. This was not always favorable. It was like ten elephants in a room – the flashing signs of silent frictions. They seemed to be in disagreements much of the time. And if that was not enough for stress on the job, the event of ALL the events happened. The supervisor decided to move his office where my husband and other personnel worked for shipping and receiving. Among other things, he played music and he played it loud. The music was unacceptable because it affected the workers greatly. The music was untasteful and a distraction to our work environment. My husband at the time kept a communion package in his desk drawer. He pulled the sacrament out of the drawer and begins to engage in prayer and communion for peace sake. He wanted God to move and do great exploits on behalf of a great work environment. Within a few days, the supervisor got a call from his boss with an assignment to another location in the company, north of the city. He had no idea, but God favored us and worked it out. A few months passed and the supervisor returned where he and my husband last worked. Order and peace is the testimony because they both became good friends and still have that relationship until this day!!! PRAISE THE LORD FOR VICTORY THROUGH THE BLOOD ☺

Chapter Eleven
Victory through the Blood: In Marriage

Marriage was instituted In the Garden of Eden when the Lord God said, "It is not good that the man should be alone; I will make him a help meet for him" (Genesis 2:18).

God had to first establish the union by speaking words to bring it to pass. The words that are spoken over a couple at the altar during a wedding ceremony are very important because they will come to pass; especially if the marriage is sealed with the blood of Jesus (the communion cup). Whatever words are spoken over a couple who get married at a courthouse come to pass as well. When we look at what the Word of God says about what He spoke over Adam and Eve, we should speak the same thing over our marriages. This is what God did and said in Genesis 1:28, God blessed them, and God said unto them, Be fruitful, and multiply, and replenish the earth, and subdue it: and have dominion over the fish of the sea, and over the fowl of the air, and over every living thing that moveth upon the earth.

If we want our marriages to be blessed, we must speak what God said over the very first marriage.

After Adam and Eve sinned in the Garden of Eden, God moved them out of their debt-free house because the spirit of disobedience was released into the land (house). But God didn't send them out of their debt-free house without the BLOOD upon their marriage, ministry or life. Genesis 3:21 says, "Unto Adam also and to his wife did the Lord God make coats of skins, and clothed them." When we sin and confess our sins, the blood of Jesus will remove them.

I am reminded in Exodus when God instructed Moses to put the blood upon the door frames of the children of Israel's houses and not to leave until the morning. The moment they put the blood on the door frames, God's protection came. When they came out of Egypt, they were debt-free and no one was sick. The BLOOD has the power to cancel debt and remove sickness. Psalms 105:37 says, "He brought them forth also with silver and gold: and there was not one feeble person among their tribes." When the church is raptured, we who are ready will leave this earth without debt, sickness, or diseases. Praise the Lord!

My husband and I are living witnesses that the blood will cancel debt. In 2007 we had a $725 debt cancelled and another creditor dropped their interest rate at the same time. Our debt was cancelled and we received favor through other creditors by honoring the BLOOD over our marriage and creditors. PRAISE THE LORD.

There is victory through the blood in marriages. When families sit, kneel, lay, or whatever position the Holy Spirit leads them to honor the communion cup (the BLOOD), change will occur in that household. You can have victory in your marriage through the BLOOD.

When husbands and wives look at what ability each other has, more will be done for that family and for the kingdom of God. God's purpose for you and your spouse is to bring the two together; not blaming one another, fussing, cursing, or fighting. Look at Adam and Eve. God put them both out of the house (Garden of Eden). God the Father sees the husband and wife as one flesh. Oneness in a marriage is essential and brings victory to the relationship.

The Holy Spirit opened my eyes to the gifts and abilities that He gave to my husband Charles. I began to tap into those gifts and abilities. I have the abilities my husband has because we are one flesh. We are a great team because of the grace of God the Father. There were times we had conflicts where we weren't agreeing on the same thing. But, now we know that agreement is a very powerful tool in marriage.

Agreements for homes, companies, children, kingdoms, and churches result in increase. Let's use Joseph and Mary for example. When Jesus was being born, what do you think might have happened if Mary wanted to have the baby in one place and Joseph wanted to have it in another place? I believe that neither the wise men nor the shepherds would have been able to find Him to worship Him. Mary might not have been in Bethlehem which was spoken of by the prophets of the Old Testament. Because Mary and Joseph were obedient to God and were both in agreement, they were blessed in abundance. As we agree with God the Father in His WORDS about our marriages we move to another dimension.

John 2:1-8: And the third day there was a marriage in Cana of Galilee; and the mother of Jesus was there. This marriage was in a specific place called Cana of Galilee. This is where people decide to get married. The kind of people that come to help celebrate is very important to the union of the husband and the wife.

[2]And both Jesus was called, and his disciples, to the marriage.

The invitation of Jesus and his disciples to the wedding served as an empowerment upon the marriage. This was the first miracle Jesus performed in Cana of Galilee, which emphasizes that Jesus agrees with marriage. If there is a situation within a marriage, Jesus can perform a miracle when we call upon the Father in His name. Jesus has done miraculous things in our marriage and still does when the house, car, money and the relationship seem to be indifferent. The Holy Spirit always steps in right on time.

[3]And when they wanted wine, the mother of Jesus saith unto him, They have no wine.

In a marriage, sometimes Jesus is the only person we need to talk to about issues to bring about a change. For example, when the wine (sweetness) at the wedding needed to be restored, the winemaker (Jesus) was present. He is always present. We must let Jesus know what needs to be restored within a marriage.

[4]Jesus saith unto her, Woman, what have I to do with thee? Mine hour is not yet come.

Jesus told His mother that it was not time to turn the water into wine yet. However, for His mother Jesus performed a miracle because she placed a demand on His anointing. Changes come when we place a demand on the anointing on the inside of us, even when it may not seem like the time to place a demand on the marriage. Sometimes we wait for the bad to turn into good; and it will as we receive God's promises.

[5]His Mother saith unto the servants. Whatsoever he saith unto you, do it.

Mary, the mother of Jesus, didn't care if it wasn't time for Jesus to do anything. She placed a demand on the anointing. She was bold as a lion, not backing down for anything. She also knew that Jesus had the ability to change anything just like He does today. All we have to do is ask the Father in His name.

Jesus says to the husband, wife and children whatsoever I say unto you do it according to my WORD. Ephesians 5:21: "Submit yourselves one to another...," Ephesians 6:1:"Children OBEY...," Ephesians 5:22:"Wives, submit yourselves unto your OWN husbands..." and Ephesians 5:25: husbands LOVE your wives..."

⁶And there were set there six water pots of stone, after the manner of the purifying of the Jews, containing two or three firkins apiece.

The water pots were waiting to be filled on the command of Jesus' mother. When we are praying for changes in our marriage, we must wait for them to be filled by Jesus who brings about the changes. Like the empty water pots at the wedding, we must also let our spouse and God the Father know that we need to be refilled.

⁷Jesus saith unto them; Fill the water pots with water. And they filled them up to the brim.

When Jesus gives instruction, it must be followed to get the results. We see that Jesus wanted marriage to have sweetness (the wine) in it, because He fulfilled a demand at the marriage. Jesus wants us to have fulfillment in our marriages.

⁸And he saith unto them, Draw out now, and bear unto the governor of the feast. And they bare it.

Jesus' second instruction was to draw out the water. As the servants drew out the water it turned into wine. If there is something going on in your marriage, draw the anointing from each other by tapping into the Holy Spirit. He will reveal your spouse's great abilities.

Let the sweet love of Jesus turn every marital issue into the sweet wine that your spouse is just your kind. The restoration of the wine at the wedding feast turned out to be greater than the wine previously served because the hand of Jesus was there to heal the brokenness. If you have been broken in your marriage and want a recharge, let the Master's hand touch you and make you whole. Sometimes in a marriage the other spouse may feel that they are right. Even if they are, they should pray for God's will to be done.

If you want to see a change in your marriage I suggest that you and your spouse honor the communion cup (the BLOOD) and see the miracle God performs in the midst.

Let's say that a spouse is expecting a change from the other spouse. The spouse with the expectation should first examine themselves and identify areas where they can change. Then, they might notice a change in their spouse. The victory is in Jesus for any changes to take place because VICTORY IS THROUGH THE BLOOD OF THE LAMB IN MARRIAGE.

When my husband and I needed a house we had to be in agreement in order to get the house. When my husband was stationed in Korea, he called me and told me that he wanted to buy a van and bring it back home. I didn't agree with him at the time, so I prayed. Even though the van was at a good price, we were in the process of paying off creditors. After my husband got off the telephone with me, the Holy Spirit asked him: "Didn't you hear what your wife said about the van?" After hanging up with him, I prayed and the Holy Spirit spoke. Wives, the Word says that our husbands may not obey the Word, but they would be won by the conversation of the wives (I Peter 3:1-6). We get better and quicker results when we pray.

Chapter Twelve
Victory over Sin through the Blood

◈

"And as they were eating, Jesus took bread, and blessed it, and brake it, and gave it to the disciples, and said, Take, eat; this is my body" –Matthew 26:26-29.

While Jesus and the disciples were eating a meal, Jesus instituted communion to illustrate how to do it and to explain the purpose of the blood. Jesus said, take and eat, for this (the bread) represents my body that is going to hang on the cross, be buried and rise on the third day.

[27]And He took the cup, and gave thanks, and gave it to them, saying, Drink ye all of it;

Here again Jesus gives another example of honoring the blood. He gave thanks and served it to His disciples.

[28]For this is my blood of the New Testament, which is shed for many for the remission of sins.

Jesus told His disciples that it was His BLOOD that was shed for the purpose of sins and that communion is a part of the New Testament ordinance. Jesus' blood remitted sins by taking them away. When doctors say that a specific disease is "in remission," they are saying that the disease has been cured. Jesus' blood was shed to cure sin.

So how do we get victory over sin in life? By accepting what the blood of Jesus did for sin. Whatever sin you want to overcome: get the communion cup, take that sin to the mercy seat (The Heavenly Father), and let the blood of Jesus cleanse you from all unrighteousness. I John 1:9 say, "If we confess our sins, he is faithful and just to forgive us our sins, and to cleanse us from all unrighteousness." Find scriptures that fit your need and honor the blood according to those scriptures.

Some say that confession is good for the soul, but we must confess to the right person. We know that God the Father is:

1.   Faithful

2.   Just to forgive us our sins because there is no sin or shadow of darkness in Him.

3.   Able to cleanse us from all unrighteousness. Not some, but all unrighteousness.

The blood of the Lamb of God was shed for every sin in the world. But what exactly is sin?

Sin is disobeying the Word of God and its commandments, statues, precepts, and standards. The Word of God is the operating procedure that we live by that is set as a guide, lamp, and principle for our lives.

Romans 6:14-15 says, "For sin shall not have dominion over you: for ye are not under the law, but under grace. What then? Shall we sin because we are not under the law, but under grace? God forbid."

We see here in the scripture that sin "shall not" —not "might not,"— have dominion over us because we are not under the law. Just because we are under grace doesn't give us a reason to sin. Being under grace, our love for God the Father should be all the more reason why we choose not to practice sin.

The next day John seeth Jesus coming unto him, and saith, Behold the Lamb of God, which taketh away the sin of the world (John 1:29).

John the Baptist made an announcement about Jesus being the Lamb of God. Perhaps some didn't know that "Jesus the

Lamb" was in their midst to remove sin. Just like the Lamb of God that was slain before the foundation of the world is in the midst of the throne of God, He is in our midst to remove our sins. In Matthew 26:28, Jesus says that His blood was shed for many for the remission of sins. The blood of Jesus was shed to remit (remove) sins and make it a New Testament agreement that anything we do can be forgiven, except blasphemy against the Holy Spirit. When we know we have sinned, we must repent by asking the Father to forgive us and honor the communion cup. I'm reminded of when Jesus honored the cup when He was betrayed by Judas Iscariot. He didn't let that stop Him, and we cannot let anything stop us. We can go to the Father in Jesus' name and He will aid us through anything. As we honor Him in everything, He will honor us when we walk in the light as He is in the light.

I John 1:7 says, "But if we walk in the light, as he is in the light, we have fellowship one with another, and the blood of Jesus Christ his son cleanseth us from all sin." When we walk in the light of the Word of God, because Jesus is the light, we have fellowship and oneness with each other just like the Father, the son and the Holy Spirit are one.

It is the blood of Jesus Christ, the son of God that cleanseth us from all sin. The blood is a cleansing agent for the Body of Christ when we confess our sins (miss the mark or the standard of the Word of God).

We cannot be condemned because Romans 8:1 tells us that, "There is therefore now no condemnation to them which are in Christ Jesus, who walk not after the flesh, but after the Spirit. "We can be cleansed from condemnation through the Blood of the Lamb. We must walk after the spirit of the Word of God so as not to fulfill the lust of the flesh.

The works of the flesh are listed in Galatians 5:19-21, and the fruit of the spirit are in Galatians 5:22-23.

Chapter Thirteen
Victory through the Blood: Overcoming Fear

This chapter will discuss the spirit of fear and how to get the victory over fear in the name of Jesus through the power of communion.

The first question we want to answer is "what is fear?"

According to Webster's Illustrated Contemporary Dictionary, fear is defined as:

1. An emotion excited by danger, evil, or pain, apprehension dread
2. Uneasiness about a thing; anxiety
3. To be afraid of
4. To be anxious about, doubtful

Many times in the Bible the angel of the Lord would have to say "fear thy not" when they would appear to people. Jesus also had to say "fear thou not," which lets us know that God doesn't want us to have the spirit of fear in Jesus' name.

Genesis 12:9-20 tells the story about how Abram was afraid of going into the country of Egypt (new territory). Entering new territory caused him to be afraid of what might happen to him. But, once he overcame the spirit of fear, it brought blessings to him and his family. Oftentimes the one thing that people are afraid of doing for the Lord is the very thing that will bring them blessings.

In 2007, I worked as a packer for a company. Once I was trained I had to tell myself to calm down and to not be anxious about anything regarding the job. I was afraid because I had been out of work for a while and wanted to work to help pay off some creditors and the Father helped me to do just that at this company. Once I let go of the fear of keeping up in a productive environment; the Lord really gave me FAVOR with the people. Praise the Lord!

Now where does fear comes from?

Fear comes from the thoughts we think that do not line up with the Word of God. Isaiah 26:3 says, "Thou wilt keep him in perfect peace, whose mind is stayed on thee: because he trusteth in thee."

Psalm 119:165:"Great peace have they which love thy law: and nothing shall offend them."

I encourage you to read this chapter in its entirety; but, Joshua 8:1 says, "And the Lord said unto Joshua, Fear not, neither be thou dismayed: take all the people of war with thee, and arise, go up to Ai: see, I have given into thy hand the king of Ai, and his people, and his city, and his land:"

God told Joshua not to fear because He had given him four things:

1. The king of Ai
2. His people
3. His city
4. His land

Fear wanted to stop Joshua from receiving from God. But, he went and obeyed God's instruction and they were truly blessed. Read the whole chapter of Joshua 8.

Isaiah 41:10, "Fear thou not; for I am with thee: be not dismayed; for I am thy God: I will strengthen thee; yea, I will help thee; yea, I will uphold thee with the right hand of my righteousness."

Philippians 4:6-9:"Be careful for nothing; but in everything by prayer and supplication with thanksgiving let your requests be made known unto God. [7]And the peace of God, which passeth all understanding, shall keep your hearts and minds through Christ

Jesus. [8]Finally, brethren, whatsoever things are true, whatsoever things are honest, whatsoever things are just, whatsoever things are pure, whatsoever things are lovely, whatsoever things are of good report; if there be any virtue, and if there be any praise, think on these things. [9]Those things, which ye have both learned, and received, and heard, and seen in me, do: and the God of peace shall be with you."

There are many more scriptures in the Bible on fear.

Fear comes from the devil who is the author of fear. But, 2 Timothy 1:7 says, "For God hath not given us the spirit of fear; but of power, and of love, and of a sound mind." If God doesn't have the spirit of fear, then we know who it comes from.

Fear can also come from people looking or hearing a situation they may be facing like Jairus, in Mark 5:22-36.

Jairus heard the words of a servant that his daughter was dead. He was about to be afraid until Jesus spoke the words: BE NOT AFRAID, ONLY BELIEVE.

When Jesus speaks, things change. Jairus acted on the words of Jesus, "be not afraid," and his daughter was brought to life again.

Fear even came upon Peter when Jesus told him to walk on the water. As Peter walked toward Jesus, he started looking at the wave and began to sink; but, the Master reached out His hand and pulled him into safety (Matthew 14:22-33).

Now let's look at how to get victory over fear through the blood:

1. First of all, we must recognize that God has not given to us the spirit of fear; but, of power, and of love and a sound mind (2 Timothy 1:7).
2. Identify the type of fear. It could be fear of love, fear of people, fear of losing, fear of fear itself, fear of worms, fear of driving, fear of spending, fear of working, fear of

doing the Word of God, fear of stepping out for the Lord, etc.

3. We must put the Word of God on the spirit of fear; because, how a person responds to fear will create an atmosphere. The atmosphere creates a climate, and a climate creates a culture. We must not respond to fear, but to the power of the blood of Jesus.

4. Take communion over the spirit of fear. Use scriptures that promise freedom like: I John 4:4; 2 Timothy 1:7; Philippians 4:13.

When honoring the communion, call out the spirit of fear along with the Word, and break the bread and drink the cup of blessing over it in the name of Jesus. Command fear to leave your life and it will. Declare a faith confession.

Who sends fear? Not God the Father because He doesn't have any to give. When we find out what something is not; then, we can easily find out what something is.

When we respond to faith, fear goes away because we cannot have faith and fear at the same time; just as we cannot serve two masters. We will love one and hate the other. We must choose (Matthew 6:24).

Here are some scriptures where the blood was offered up and life came.

Read Genesis 4:4-7. Abel brought God his best gift: a blood sacrifice, which caused him to be accepted. Cain's offering was not accepted because he did not offer blood to God. We are accepted in the beloved by Jesus Christ's blood (Ephesians 1:6).

Read Genesis 8:18-22. When Noah came out of the ark after the flood, he built God an altar and offered a blood sacrifice. God was well pleased when the blood was offered. It brought some promises to the earth:

1. *A rainbow was established forever. When we see a rainbow, we are reminded that God promised not to destroy the earth anymore with a flood.*
2. *God said there will always be season plus day and night as long as the earth remains.*

In 1 Kings 3:1-15, King Solomon offered up the blood sacrifice with one thousand burnt offerings and God appeared to him in a dream and granted him anything he wanted.

Read Colossians 2:13-15. When Jesus spoiled powers and principalities, He made a shew of them openly and gained sons and daughters into His kingdom.

Read Colossians 1:13-14.Through the blood we have been delivered from the power of darkness and translated into the kingdom of His dear son.

✠FAITH CONFESSION✠

By the blood of the Lamb
I look to the Great I AM
The blood cleanses from all sins
By the blood I can enter in
The power is in the blood
Therefore I have no worry
God has not given me the spirit of fear
By the blood I can see clear
I can live without fear

By the blood of Jesus I can hear, in Jesus' name.

Chapter Fourteen

Victory through the Blood: in Finances

I want to open this chapter with a personal testimony. In 2003-2006, my husband Charles and I were challenged in our finances while in Riverdale, Georgia. The Father kept telling me that He would restore everything that was lost and I believed Him because when God speaks, His words will come to pass.

When our Sable car was repossessed, God the Father had a ram in the bush. Pastors gave us a car; then, another person gave us a truck and we were very thankful to God the Father for their obedience. The reason why I said "God the Father" is because the scripture says that we can do nothing without Jesus' help (John 15:5).

We had those two cars until December 5, 2007 when the Holy Spirit led us to the Toyota dealership in McDonough, Georgia. I had a 2007 Camry in mind, but we got a brand new 2008 Toyota Corolla. The miraculous thing about it was that my husband only had a pay stub for $14.47 from a job he had just started in McDonough and I wasn't working at the time. The day we went to the dealership was called Hanukkah Day, which represents a candle burning of continuous prayer (miracle day). Truly a miracle happened.

My husband's name was put on the car title with only a pay stub of $14.47 and we drove away with the car the next day. After having the car, we received four letters informing us that the car was not approved, but we were already driving the evidence of the car. The Father told me that He is bigger than bankruptcy and repossession. He proved that when we drove off the car lot in a 2008 Toyota Corolla that no one had ever owned. Some may think, "what's so good about a New 2008 Corolla? "Well, if I can be transparent, our receiving any car after having gone through credit issues is a good thing. We give glory to God the Father!!!!!

According to Galatians 3:13-14, *Christ hath redeemed us from the curse of the law, being made a curse for us: for it is written, Cursed is every one that hangeth on a tree: [14]That the blessing of Abraham might come on the Gentiles through Jesus Christ; that we might receive the promise of the spirit through faith.*

What curse did Christ redeem us from?
1. Spiritual death
2. Poverty and lack
3. Sicknesses and diseases

Christ has redeemed us from poverty. He is not "going to" redeem us because He has already broken the curse of poverty and given us the spirit of wealth and riches that we must accept into our lives.

What is the spirit of poverty?

According to Webster's Illustrated Contemporary Dictionary, *poverty* is
(1) The state of being poor, need
(2) Scarcity of something needed
(3) Meagerness; inadequacy

Poor is defined as
(1) lacking means of comfortable sustenance; needy
(2) Lacking in good qualities
(3) Wanting in strength or spirit cowardly.

In other words, Christ has redeemed us from the spirit of poverty because He became poor so that we, the Body of Christ, can become rich (Galatians 3:13-14).

The blood removed the spirit of poverty that was on the cross when Christ shed His precious blood at the cross.

Poverty is a curse, but Christ was made a curse for us. For it is written, "Cursed is every one that hangeth on a tree:" Christ took the place of poverty and gave us wealth, an exchange in the blood covenant. Jesus' strength took away our weakness that the blessing of Abraham would come on the Gentiles through Jesus Christ (the blood); that we might receive the promise of the spirit through faith.

These are the blessings that God promised Abram in Genesis 12:1-3:

1. A land that He would shew him.
2. To make him a great nation
3. To bless him and make his name great and that he shall be a blessing
4. To bless those that bless him and curse those who curse him and in him shall all families of the earth be blessed. Abram obeyed.

In Genesis 17:5-8 these are the promises God made to Abraham after He changed his name:

1. God established a covenant with Abraham
2. Abraham shall be a father of many nations
3. Abraham will be "exceeding fruitful"
4. Abraham shall birth nations and kings
5. God established an everlasting covenant with Abraham and his seed to be a God to them all

6. God gave Abraham and his seed the land where they were strangers, all the land of Canaan for an everlasting possession.

Look at the differences in blessings that the name Abram received verses Abraham. Abram received about four blessings, where Abraham received six or more blessings.

✗ FAITH CONFESSION ✗

Father, by the blood of Jesus; you have made me righteous and accepted through the blood of Jesus.

By the blood of Jesus, I am blessed and highly favored by You.

By the blood of Jesus, I am the object of Your affection.

Your favor surrounds me like a shield. The first thing people come into contact with is my favor shield.

By the blood, I have favor with You, Father, and man today.

All day long people go out of their way to bless me and to help me.

I have favor with everyone that I deal with today.

By the blood of Jesus, doors that were once closed are now opened for me.

By the blood of Jesus I receive preferential treatment. I have special privileges and I am God's favorite child.

By the blood of Jesus, no good thing will He withhold from me.

Because of God's favor, my enemies cannot triumph over me.

By the blood of Jesus, I have supernatural increase and promotion.

By the Blood of Jesus, I declare restoration of everything that the devil has stolen from me.

By the blood Jesus, I have honor in the midst of my adversaries and an increase of assets, and land.

By the blood of Jesus, I am highly favored by God. I experience great victories, supernatural increase and miraculous breakthrough in the midst circumstances.

I receive supernatural recognition, prominence and honor. Petitions are granted to me by the favor of God.

I win battles because God fights them for me. This is the day; the set and designated time to experience the favors of God that profusely and lavishly abound in my life, In Jesus' name, Amen.

After the confessions, let's explore some examples in the Word of God where the blood of the Lamb was applied in the midst of the adversary and achieved victories.

Exodus 12:12, "For I will pass through the land of Egypt this night, and will smite all the firstborn in the land of Egypt, both man and beast; and against all the gods of Egypt I will execute judgment: I am the Lord."

God said that He will pass through the land of Egypt at night to smite all of Egypt's firstborn and that is what He did.

Verse 13: And the blood shall be to you for a token upon the houses where ye are: and when I see the blood, I will pass over you, and the plague shall not be upon you to destroy you, when I smite the land of Egypt.

God said that the blood shall be, not might be, a token (sign) upon the houses of the children of Israel; and when God saw the blood on the houses, the plague (sicknesses and diseases) did not come upon them or destroy them.

God wants the anointing to flow out of our homes and anywhere else. Most of us don't have something going on at church or at the job like we do at home.

We know that the destroyer did not destroy the houses that had the blood of the Lamb upon them, no matter who was in the house. God stated that He was looking for the blood; which means that God still looks for the blood of the Lamb to be on our natural homes and our spiritual hearts. Hallelujah, the plague or the destroyer will not stay in our homes because the blood is on our doors.

[14] And this day shall be unto you for a memorial; and ye shall keep it a feast to the Lord throughout your generations; ye shall keep it a feast by an ordinance forever.

God gave Moses instruction to give to the children of Israel to keep the Passover feast throughout their generation. The Passover feast was a set time to celebrate how the blood delivered them from the hand of the death angel. The feast was to be honored in their homes, and they were to keep it as an ordinance forever, even when they crossed over into the Promised Land. The keeping of the Passover was so essential that Jesus honored it just before He was crucified.

The children of Israel came out of Egypt debt-free to serve their God, and the Egyptians were glad they were gone. We also have been set free by the blood of Jesus to serve the living God our Father.

2 Corinthians 8:9:"For ye know the grace of our Lord Jesus Christ, that, though he was rich, yet for your sakes he became poor, that ye through his poverty might be rich."

We became rich when Jesus came to the earth, because there is no spirit of poverty in heaven; but, a spirit of wealth and riches. We must claim our inheritance in Jesus' name.

Psalm 112:3 says, "Wealth and riches shall be in his house: and his righteousness endureth forever..." to those who follow the commandments. The reason why "wealth and riches are in his house" is found in verse 1: he/she delighteth greatly in the Father's commandments (instruction).

Let's look at King Solomon and the victory he received when he offered up the blood sacrifice.

[1 Kings 3:3] And Solomon loved the Lord, walking in the statutes of David his father: only he sacrificed and burnt incense in high places." Solomon loved the Lord and walked in the statues (ways) of his father David. Solomon offered burnt incense and sacrifices in the high places while David his father offered them somewhere else.

[4] And the king went to Gibeon to sacrifice there; for that was the great high place: a thousand burnt offerings did Solomon offer upon the altar."

King Solomon went to a specific place called Gibeon, the great high place, to do his sacrifice. He offered a thousand burnt offerings upon the altar (a blood sacrifice). In our lives as Christians; we must choose a place to meet the Heavenly Father daily.

[5] In Gibeon the Lord appeared to Solomon in a dream by night: and God said, ask what I shall give thee."

The blood brought King Solomon victory. He was able to ask God for anything he wanted because he offered up to God what He wanted, which was the blood. When we honor communion cup, the Holy Spirit will reveal things to us to enhance our growth in the kingdom of His Dear Son.

Even though King Solomon is not listed in the hall of faith (the book of Hebrews), he still did a great work for God and his people.

This next victory about the river that looked like the blood from the scriptures is very interesting because the enemy was once again defeated.

2 Kings 3:20:"And it came to pass in the morning, when the meat offering was offered, that, behold, there came water by the way of Edom, and the country was filled with water."

The prophet Elisha gives a prophetic word about the water that will fill the valley, defeat the enemies, and reap great spoils for God's people. When the blood sacrifice was offered up, water seemly came from everywhere to fill the valley.

21 And when all the Moabites heard that the kings were come up to fight against them, they gathered all that were able to put on armour, and upward, and stood, in the border.

When the Moabites heard that the kings were coming together to fight them, they gathered all that were able to put on armor to fight.

22-23 And they rose up early in the morning, and the sun shone upon the water, and the Moabites saw the water on the other side as red as blood: And they said, this is blood: the kings are surely slain, and they have smitten one another: now therefore, Moab, to the spoil.

When the Moabites rose up early in the morning, the sun shined on the water that it made it look red like blood. They persuaded each other to go toward what they thought was red water. It only looked red so the enemies went to get the spoil; but, was defeated. They said this is blood.

24 And when they came to the camp of Israel, the Israelites rose up and smote the Moabites, so that they fled before them:

but they went forward smiting the Moabites, even in their country.

Because the water turned into blood, the Israelites defeated the Moabites so greatly that they caused them to go back to their own country to be smitten.

[25]And they beat down the cities, and on every good piece of land cast every man his stone, and filled it; and they stopped all the wells of water, and felled all the good trees: only in Kir-haraseth left they the stones thereof; howbeit the slingers went about it, and smote it.

Israel destroyed the cities of the Moabites, stopped up their wells of water and cut down their trees. They left the land of Kir-haraseth alone until the slingers smote them also.

[26 - 27]When the king of Moab saw that the battle was too intense for him, he took 700 men to break through to the king of Edom but he could not. He took his eldest son and offered him up as a blood sacrifice on the wall. That caused Israel to depart from him and return to their land. So the blood gave victory over the enemy at the end!!!!!!

VICTORY IS IN THE BLOOD.

Chapter Fifteen
Victory through the Blood: in Ministry

Victory in ministry with the blood began with Adam and Eve. Their ministry was to tend the garden. Their sin dismissed them from God's presence, so they hid themselves from ministry until the blood clothed them. Their disobedience led them out of their assignment of the garden and to another assignment.

Unto Adam also and to his wife did the Lord God make coats of skins, and clothed them (Genesis 3:21).

God had to reestablish Adam and Eve's purpose after they went beyond the boundaries that He had set up for them. As a result, God had to kill an animal to offer a blood sacrifice on Adam and Eve's behalf. God not only killed the blood sacrifice for them; but, also clothed them in the blood sacrifice.

This is the first place written in the scriptures where blood was shed. God started with the blood in the garden, and ended with the blood through Jesus Christ, also known as the second Adam.

When a man and woman join together in holy matrimony, Holy Communion should be served at the wedding because this man and woman are starting their assignment in ministry. At the ceremony they make a blood covenant with each other, God the Father, and the family members on both sides. Remember Jesus' first miracle was turning water into wine at a marriage celebration (John 2).

My husband and I have discovered how important it is to keep the bloodline over, around, in and before us in our home, ministry and workplaces and wherever we go. We discovered the importance of the blood or taking communion on a daily basis in 1996. However, it wasn't until 1998 when we really understood the blood's power over death during my near death experience.

We thank God for the blood of the Lamb upon our lives. The Lamb of God was slain for us over 2,000 years ago.

Now back to Adam and Eve; they got victory through the blood because they went out of the garden clothed in the blood.

Elijah received his victory through the blood in his ministry when he demonstrated the power of the blood sacrifice with the prophets of Baal.

> *And Elijah came unto all the people, and said, how long halt ye between two opinions? if the Lord be God, follow him: but if Baal, then follow him. And the people answered him not a word. Then said Elijah unto the people, I, even I only, remain a prophet of the Lord; but Baal's prophets are four hundred and fifty men. Let them therefore give us two bullocks; and let them choose one bullock for themselves, and cut it in pieces, and lay it on wood, and put no fire under: and I will dress the other bullock, and lay it on wood, and put no fire under:* (I Kings 18:21-23)

Elijah came to the children of Israel through the sacrifice of the bullocks. He wanted the people to see that whenever the true prophets use the blood there will be victory. The blood brought about a decision to be made as to who the true and living God is. The blood did it. Hallelujah!!!!!

The book of Acts tells us that the Apostles had victory in their ministries because they took the things that Jesus taught them and left a legacy for the next generation about honoring the bread and the fruit of the cup (the blood).

Jesus' apostles were like his staff that learned about the importance of honoring the blood. Even in the midst of training, Jesus was betrayed by one of His staff members, and the bread and the blood gave enlightenment about who the enemy was. The apostles had the heart of the Father to teach the people about communion which is why so many people were being saved back then. The spirit, the water, and the blood agree here on the earth. (I John 5:8)

Whenever the blood is honored, the Holy Spirit will show up. *Then they that gladly received his word were baptized: and the same day there were added unto them about three thousand souls* (Acts 2:41).

Those 3,000 souls who received the word from the apostles were glad and baptized.

Verse [42]*And they continued steadfastly in the apostle's doctrine and fellowship, and in breaking of bread, and in prayers.*

Those who were taught by the Apostles didn't go to the right or the left. They stayed in the teachings of the Word of God that they heard in fellowship, in the breaking of bread (communion) and in prayers.

These four areas are very important to the Body of Christ:

1. Doctrine (teaching of the apostles)
2. Fellowship
3. Breaking of bread (communion)
4. Prayers

[43]*And fear came upon every soul: and many wonders and signs were done by the apostles.*

As an apostle myself, having traveled to different places, signs and wonders were performed through my hands by the grace of God. Once, the Lord told me to give a person $2 and they received a promotion on their job. I gave a person $3 and they received a large sum of money. I laid hands on people who were sick, or just spoke the Word of God over their lives, and nose bleeds stopped, tumors disappeared and cancer dried up by the roots.

44-45 And all that believed were together, and had all things common; And sold their possessions and goods, and parted them to all men, as every man had need.

The people were together and believed the same thing and unselfishly sold their possessions and goods so that every man's needs were met.

46-47 And they, continuing daily with one accord in the temple, and breaking bread from house to house, did eat their meat with gladness and singleness of heart, Praising God, and having favour with all the people. And the Lord added to the church daily such as should be saved.

Key points in verses 46 & 47:

1. **The people continued daily with one accord in the temple.** When we as the body of Christ come together on one accord, signs, wonders, miracles, and mighty deeds will increase in the church (the Body of Christ) and around the world.
2. **They broke bread from house to house with gladness (not sadness) and singleness (one purpose in mind) of heart.**
3. **Praising God vs. complaining to God.** When we praise we raise; when we complain, we remain.
4. **The people's praises released God's favor and the Lord added (not subtracted) to the church DAILY such as should be saved.** Everyday people were added to the Body of Christ through salvation.

On January 16, 1977, I was added to the Body of Christ (the church) in Shape, Belgium. As the congregation praised God during a Sunday night service, the Lord drew me into His kingdom for His purposes and plans for my life to glorify Him. Nothing can pluck me out of His hands. Hallelujah!

Chapter Sixteen
Victory through the Blood: Generational Blessings

❧⊗❧

Generational blessings are often referred to as something that has been passed through a lineage. Jesus Christ, for example, passed to us His life through the shedding of His precious blood to Abraham and on down through generations to us.

Ephesians 1:3 says, "Blessed be the God and Father of our Lord Jesus Christ, who hath blessed us with all spiritual blessings..."

Apostle Paul told the church of Ephesus that the blessings have already been spoken over our lives. Where are these blessings coming from? Blessings come from God the Father and the Lord Jesus Christ our Savior. We are blessed (empowered to prosper) with all, not some, but all spiritual blessings.

Here are some examples in the Bible where the blessings were spoken over the lives of people:

Example 1: Genesis 1:26-28: And God said, Let us make man in our image, after our likeness: and let them have dominion over the fish of the sea, and over the fowl of the air, and over the cattle, and over all the earth, and over every creeping thing that creepeth upon the earth.

God had to say something first ("Let us make") to create something else ("man in our image"). God said that man would have dominion over the fish, the fowls, the cattle, all the earth, and everything that creepeth upon the earth.

Verse 27: So God created man in his own image, in the image of God created he him; male and female created he them.

God created us (man) so we have creativity inside of us to come on the outside of us (man) because we are in the image of God. God made male and female; not, man and man; or, woman and woman; but, male and female. He connected male and female together like love bugs; staying connected together, even when the love bugs are flying around.

Verse 28: And God blessed them, and God said unto them, Be fruitful, and multiply, and replenish the earth, and subdue it: and have dominion over the fish of the sea, and over the fowl of the air, and over every living thing that moveth upon the earth.

God prophesied the following life and blessings over Adam, Eve and the generations to come:

1. Be fruitful
2. Multiply
3. Replenish the earth
4. Subdue the earth
5. Have dominion over the fish of the sea
6. Have dominion over the fowl of the air
7. Have dominion over every living thing that moves upon the earth.

Example 2: Genesis 4:25, 26: And Adam knew his wife again; and she bare a son, and called his name Seth: For God, said she, hath appointed me another seed instead of Abel, whom Cain slew.

God prophesied that Seth was his appointed seed after Cain slew Abel. We, who are born again, are God's appointed seed.

26 And to Seth, to him also there was born a son; and he called his name Enos: then began men to call upon the name of the Lord.

After God spoke destiny over Seth, there was a release for men to call upon the name of the Lord.

Examples 3: While working at a company that was experiencing cuts, some people were let go, but not me. I believed that there was a generation within the company who must have known about Jesus Christ. I consider that a blessing from the Father. God spoke words over me that I am blessed going in and blessed going out. I claimed the promise, therefore I was blessed to stay until the company closed its doors.

Example 4: Genesis 9:1, 2: And God blessed Noah and his sons, and said unto them, be fruitful, and multiply, and replenish the earth. [2]And the fear of you and the dread of you shall be upon every beast of the earth, and upon every fowl of the air, upon all that moveth upon the earth, and upon all the fishes of the sea; into your hand are they delivered.

God blessed Noah and his sons. He told them to be fruitful, to multiply, to replenish the earth and to not fear the animals. God put a certain fear in the relationship between the animals and Noah and his family.

Generational blessings are also found in the New Testament.

I Corinthians 10:16: The cup of blessing which we bless, is it not the communion of the blood of Christ? The bread which we break, is it not the communion of the body of Christ?

The blood of Christ is what causes the cup to bring continual blessings. Just like we naturally drink from a cup or glass daily, we can drink from the power of the blood of Christ daily.

The bread that we break comes into union with the Body of Christ daily. Just like we eat from our natural table every day, with the exception of fasting and praying, we can eat from the table of the Lord every day. We need to look for blessings daily. Psalm 68:19 says, "Blessed be the Lord, who daily loadeth us with benefits; even the God of our salvation. Selah."

Christ hath redeemed us from the curse of the law, being made a curse for us: for it is written, Cursed is every one that hangeth on a tree: That the blessing of Abraham might come on the Gentiles through Jesus Christ; that we might receive the promise of the Spirit through faith (Galatians 3:13, 14).

Christ has already redeemed us from the curse of the law which includes: spiritual death, poverty and lack, sickness, and disease. Jesus Christ took the curse for us and placed it on Himself that the blessings of Abraham will be upon us. Read about the blessings of Abraham in Genesis 12: 1-3.

What are the blessings of Abraham that we can receive?
+ Land that God will show us
+ To be a great nation
+ To be blessed
+ A name made great
+ To be a blessing
+ People are blessed when they bless us
+ People are cursed when they curse us
+ All families of the earth shall be blessed through us
+ Obedience to follow the instruction that is given for the blessing

Now, let's look at Revelation 1:3 and how blessed we are when we read the Word (will) of God.

Blessed is he that readeth, and they that hear the words of this prophecy, and keep those things which are written therein: for the time is at hand.

We are blessed when we read the Words of the Heavenly Father; and we are blessed (empowered) to prosper when we hear the Word of the Heavenly Father. Read Deuteronomy 28:1-14 and claim the blessings in those scriptures.

77

And after eight days again his disciples were within, and Thomas with them: then came Jesus, the doors being shut, and stood in the midst, and said, Peace be unto you. (John 20:26).

Jesus came and spoke the blessing of peace upon the disciples after He was raised from death. His words are a generational blessing that will last for eternity.

Here are more scriptures on generational blessings:

Proverbs 10:22 says, "The blessing of the Lord, it maketh rich, and he addeth no sorrow with it." The Lord brings blessings of richness and there will not be any sorrow with it.

Proverbs 28:20 says, "A faithful man shall abound with blessings: but he that maketh haste to be rich shall not be innocent." Be faithful (obedient) to God the Father and He shall cause blessings to abound.

Malachi 3:10 says, "Bring ye all the tithes into the storehouse, that there may be meat in mine house, and prove me now herewith, saith the Lord of hosts, if I will not open you the windows of heaven, and pour you out a blessing, that there shall not be room enough to receive it."

When you bring your tithes into the storehouse, there is resource in the storehouse, and you will reap blessings.

James 3:10 says, "Out of the same mouth proceedeth blessing and cursing. My brethren, these things ought not so to be." Speaking the right blessings out of our mouths brings blessings.

Revelation 5:12 says, "Saying with a loud voice, Worthy is the Lamb that was slain to receive power, and riches, and wisdom, and strength, and honour, and glory, and blessing."

When we say with a loud voice," Worthy is the Lamb", that brings power, riches, wisdom, strength, honor, glory, and blessings into our lives through the Blood of the Lamb. We are using the seven facets of the anointing, because there is VICTORY in the BLOOD.

Chapter Seventeen
Victory through the Blood: Having Good Health

III John 1:2: "Beloved, I wish above all things that thou mayest prosper and be in health, even as thy soul prospereth."

Here Apostle John is telling us that God the Father wants us to be in health as our soul prospers.

My soul prospered so much on the blood of the Lamb in 1998. It was amazing how quick the Lord allowed me to recover from a near death situation with fibroid tumors. The Father kept me and continues to keep me.

I'd like to give an assignment for health and healing in this chapter. Remember, each time God's instruction was followed in the Bible; there was a manifestation of health or some sort of blessing.

Webster's Dictionary defines "health" and "healing" as the following:

Health soundness of body or mind; well-being

    ✝ Wholesome; nothing missing or nothing broken
    ✝ Strong
    ✝ Vigorous

Healing to restore to health or soundness

- ✝ Make well again
- ✝ To cause the cure or recovery of a wound injury
- ✝ To free from grief, worry, etc.
- ✝ To perform a cure or cures.

Here is the instruction: all of the health and healing scriptures are listed below from the Bible. They are available for you to read, meditate on, memorize, visualize, personalize, write, preach, and teach or anything else the Holy Spirit leads you to do. You can write them, highlight them in your Bible, confess them and honor the blood according to them. Here are a few examples of scriptures on "health" and confessing them:

17 Health Scriptures

Genesis 43:28: And they answered, Thy servant our father is in good health, he is yet alive. And they bowed down their heads, and made obeisance.

CONFESSION

Heavenly Father, I thank you that I am in good health and I worship you according to the blood covenant for my good health through this bread and blood in Jesus' name.

2 Samuel 20:9: And Joab said to Amasa, Art thou in health, my brother? And Joab took Amasa by the beard with the right hand to kiss him.

✂CONFESSION✂

Thank You Father for you cause me to be in good health. By the bread and the blood I keep my good health in Jesus' name.

Psalm 42:11: *Why art thou cast down, O my soul? and why art thou disquieted within me? Hope thou in God: for I shall yet praise him, who is the health of my countenance, and my God.*

✂CONFESSION✂

God the Father is the health of my countenance and I shall yet praise Him through the Blood of Jesus.

Here are more scriptures on health and healing that you can study.

Health

1. Genesis 43:28
2. II Samuel 20:9
3. Psalm 42:11
4. Psalm 43:5
5. Psalm 67:2
6. Proverbs 3:8
7. Proverbs 4:22
8. Proverbs 12:18
9. Proverbs 13:17
10. Proverbs 16:24
11. Isaiah 58:8
12. Jeremiah 8:15
13. Jeremiah 8:22
14. Jeremiah 30:17
15. Jeremiah 33:6
16. Acts 27:34
17. 3 John 1:2

Heal

1. Numbers 12: 3	14. Jeremiah 17:14	27. Mark 3:15
2. Deuteronomy 32:39	15. Jeremiah 30:17	28. Luke 4:18
3. 2 Kings 20:5	16. Lamentations 2:13	29. Luke 4:23
4. 2 Kings 20:8	17. Hosea 5:13	30. Luke 5:17
5. 2 Chronicles 7:14	18. Hosea 6:1	31. Luke 6:7
6. Psalms 6:2	19. Hosea 14:4	32. Luke 7:3
7. Psalm 41:4	20. Zechariah 11:6	33. Luke 9:2
8. Psalm 60:2	21. Matthew 8:7	34. Luke 10:9
9. Ecclesiastes 3:3	22. Matthew 10:1	35. Luke 14:3
10. Isaiah 19:22	23. Matthew 10:8	36. John 4:47
11. Isaiah 57:18	24. Matthew 12:10	37. John 12:40
12. Isaiah 57:19	25. Matthew 13:15	38. Acts 4:30
13. Jeremiah 3:22	26. Mark 3:2	39. Acts 28:27

Healer

1. Isaiah 3:7

Healeth

1. Exodus 15:26
2. Psalm 103:3
3. Psalm 147:3
4. Isaiah 30:26

Healing

1. Jeremiah 14:19	8. Luke 9:11
2. Jeremiah 30:13	9. Acts 4:22
3. Nahum 3:19	10. Acts10:38
4. Malachi 4:2	11. I Corinthians 12:9
5. Matthew 4:23,24	12. I Corinthians 12:30
6. Matthew 9:35	13. Revelation 22:2
7. Luke 9:6	

Juanita L. Ford

Healings

1. I Corinthians 12:28

Healed

1. Genesis 20:17
2. Exodus 21:19
3. Leviticus 13:19
4. Leviticus 14:48
5. Leviticus 14: 48
6. Deuteronomy 28:27
7. Deuteronomy 28:35
8. I Samuel 6:3
9. 2 Kings 2:21, 22
10. 2 Kings 8:29
11. 2 Kings 9:15
12. 2 Chronicles 22:6`
13: 2 Chronicles 30:20
14. Psalm 30:2
15. Psalm 107:20
16. Isaiah 53:5

17. Jeremiah 8:11
18. Jeremiah 6: 14
19. Jeremiah 15:18
20. Jeremiah 17:14
21. Jeremiah 51:9
22. Jeremiah 52:8
23. Ezekiel 30:21
24. Ezekiel 34:4
25. Ezekiel 47:8, 9, 11
26. Hosea 7:1
27. Hosea 11:23
28. Matthew: 4:24
29. Matthew 8:8, 13, 16
30. Matthew 12:15, 22
31. Matthew 14:14
32. Matthew 15:30

Scriptures Continued
Healed

33. Matthew 19:2	49. Luke 8:43
34. Matthew 21:14	50. Luke 8:47
35. Mark 1:34	51. Luke 9:11
36. Mark 3:10	52. Luke 9:42
37. Mark 5:23	53. Luke 13:14
38. Mark 5:29	54. Luke 14:4
39. Mark 6:5	55. Luke 17:15
40. Mark 6:13	56. Luke 22:51
41. Luke 4:40	57. John 5:13
42. Luke 5:15	58. Acts 3:11
43. Luke 6:17	59. Acts 4:14
44. Luke 6:18	60. Acts 5:16
45. Luke 6:19	61. Acts8:7
46. Luke 7:7	62. Acts 14:9
47. Luke 8:2	63. Acts 28:8,9
48. Luke 8:36	64. Hebrews 12:13
	65. James 5:16
	66. I Peter 2:24
	67. Revelation 13:3
	68. Revelation 13:12

Here is a daily 𝕏 CONFESSION 𝕏

I stay in good health and am healed by the Blood of Jesus the Lamb. I overcome Satan (sickness or disease) by the word of my testimony and the Word of God the Father.

Stay blessed, healthy, wealthy, and wise in Jesus name.

Chapter Eighteen
Victory in the Blood: Having Faith

Having faith in the blood means to put our trust in what the blood did for us through Jesus Christ.

Whom God hath set forth to be a propitiation through faith in his blood, to declare his righteousness for the remission of sins that are past, through the forbearance of God; To declare, I say, at this time his righteousness: that he might be just, and the justifier of him which believeth in Jesus (Romans 3:25, 26).

Jesus became a substitute for us; so we must put our trust in His blood that He shed for us. We are to declare His righteousness so that our sins (past, present and future) can be remitted.

Hebrews 11:28 says, "Through faith [Moses] kept the Passover, and the sprinkling of blood, lest he that destroyed the firstborn should touch them. "Moses put his faith in the blood when God instructed the children of Israel to put the blood on their doorposts and side posts.

I put my faith in the blood because of what the Bible says about what the blood did for me. I know it works. It gives me victory in every area of my life.

Exodus 12:6, 7, *and ye shall keep it up until the fourteenth day of the same month: and the whole assembly of the congregation of*

Israel shall kill it in the evening. And they shall take of the blood, and strike it on the two side posts and on the upper door post of the houses, wherein they shall eat it.

The Israelites put their faith in the blood when Moses gave the instruction to put the blood on their doorposts in preparation of their deliverance from Egypt. They prayed for deliverance and God did just what He promised. Since they put their faith in the blood, the Israelites knew the power of the blood would prevent the destroyer from entering their homes to destroy them.

When Israel put the blood on their doors, they believed God for the miraculous to happen. The miraculous only happened through obedience, putting faith in the blood, and knowing that it would do what it is designed to do.

We put our faith in the blood every day, evening, and night and we are seeing the miraculous happen. In November-December 2007 my husband and I worked for a company. My husband started as a temporary employee; but, in March 2008 he was hired permanently. After he was hired permanently, we put our faith in the blood for a promotion and he was moved to an office position. I was also moved from a packing to an auditing position. Even when jobs were cut, the Lord allowed me to work until the company closed. We put our faith in the blood and the blood did it.

Some may ask if the blood works in any situation. Since the blood worked on a doorpost, surely it will work on your situation. When you seek first the kingdom of God all these things are being added to you in abundance.

Through faith in the blood of Jesus, I went to a wisdom conference and received favor in getting free books and special seating.

Revelation 12:11: *And they overcame him (Satan) by the blood of the Lamb and by the word of their testimony; and they loved not their lives unto the death.*

I've come to know that in every situation we overcome Satan in everything by the blood of the Lamb and the word of our testimony. The blood is what defeated Satan a long time ago and the blood is still defeating him because it will never lose it power.

There is power in the blood and the Body of Christ is getting more revelation of the healing power of the blood.

According to Hebrews 9:19-22: *For when Moses had spoken every precept to all the people according to the law, he took the blood of calves and of goats, with water, and scarlet wool, and hyssop, and sprinkled both the book and all the people, Saying, This is the blood of the testament which God hath enjoined unto you. Moreover he sprinkled with blood both the tabernacle, and all the vessels of the ministry. And almost all things are by the law purged with blood; and without shedding of blood is no remission.*

Here is the revelation God the Father showed me in these verses:

1.   Before I study the Word of God, I honor the blood to give me life and revelation. When I study God's Word my eyes will be opened with revelation knowledge of Him according to Ephesians 1:17-21 and Psalm 119:18.

2.   When I hear a great prophetic word from the Father through the men and women of God preaching, I seal the word with the blood of Jesus the Lamb. I meditate on the word, plead the Blood on my right ear, because that was the anointing custom in the Old Testament (for the prophets?), and apply it to my life.

3. Before I preach or teach, I will either plead the blood seven times or say something about the blood.

4. I plead the blood over things and family because Moses sprinkled the blood on the book and all the people.

5. Moses also sprinkled blood on the tabernacle and all the vessels of the ministry.

6. Keep the blood in your daily dealings.

Chapter Nineteen
Victory through Sprinkling the Blood

The word "sprinkling" in the Webster Illustrated Contemporary Dictionary means
  (1) Scatter in drops or small particles and
  (2) Scatter over or upon.

Why should we sprinkle the blood?
1. Because God saw a need or had a vision for the blood to be sprinkled on the altar, on something or someone.
2. Miracles happen when the blood is sprinkled. Exodus 9:8 says, "And the Lord said unto Moses and unto Aaron, Take to you handfuls of ashes of the furnace, and let Moses sprinkle it toward the heaven in the sight of Pharaoh." When they sprinkled the ashes something happened.
3. Sprinkling the blood seals a covenant and spoken words. Read Hebrews 9:18-21

When we think about sprinkling the blood of Jesus from our mouth, something supernatural happens because death and life is in the power of the tongue. The old and new covenant scriptures refer to sprinkling the blood to let us know that just as we anoint things with oil for certain reasons, we can also sprinkle the blood for those same reasons.

Let's look at the scripture in Exodus at the beginning of the chapter. Even though it refers to sprinkling ashes instead of the blood, something still happened in the heavenly realms when the instruction was given and obeyed.

The Lord instructed Moses and Aaron to take a handful of ashes and sprinkle it into the heaven. Moses sprinkled the ashes in front of Pharaoh so he could see a miracle with his own eyes.

Exodus 9:9 says, "And it shall become small dust in all the land of Egypt, and shall be a boil breaking forth with blains upon man, and upon beast, throughout all the land of Egypt."

What was the purpose of sprinkling the ashes toward heaven? So that the supernatural power of God would come forth and the boil (curses) would come on the people and the animals of Egypt because of Pharaoh's refusal to let God's people go.

Exodus 9:10 *And they took ashes of the furnace, and stood before Pharaoh; and Moses sprinkled it up toward heaven; and it became a boil breaking forth with blains upon man, and upon beast.*

Moses and the furnace ashes remind me of the three Hebrew boys in the fiery furnace. Just like things put in a furnace get hot, so something was about to get hot with Pharaoh and his kingdom. Moses' instruction to sprinkle the ashes didn't make sense to Pharaoh (the world system), but because God said it, the boils manifested for him to see God's power.

Exodus 9:11 *And the magicians could not stand before Moses because of the boils; for the boil was upon the magicians, and upon all the Egyptians.*

When the ashes were sprinkled by the men of God (Moses and Aaron), the world system (Pharaoh and his kingdom) could not stand against the power of God. It is when we plead the blood over Satan that we overcome him by the word of our testimony about what the blood has already done for us in Jesus name. Hallelujah!

Exodus 29:15 *Thou shalt also take one ram; and Aaron and his sons shall put their hands upon the head of the ram.*

The verse above was God's instruction to Aaron and his sons, the priests. The priests at that time were the only ones allowed to lay hands. Notice that Moses didn't lay his hands on the head of the ram because that wasn't his assignment. He delegated Aaron and his sons to the office of the priest, because they were anointed for that office.

Exodus 29: 16 *And thou shalt slay the ram and thou shalt take his blood, and sprinkle it round about upon the altar.*

Aaron and his sons were to slay the ram and sprinkle the blood around the altar. I grew up in a Methodist Church and I remember how the congregation used to come to the altar in groups and honor the blood on the first Sunday of each month. I thank God that they still honor the blood covenant to this day.

What is so significant about the altar? It is a place where worship was established and where the blood of sacrifices was sprinkled. We thank God that Jesus was the ultimate sacrifice for us. We have no need to sprinkle the blood of slain animals today. What we can do now is plead the blood. In this Exodus chapter, there is no specific number of times mentioned to sprinkle the blood. In other scriptures; however, the blood was sprinkled seven times.

Exodus 29:17 *And thou shalt cut the ram in pieces, and wash the inwards of him, and his legs, and put them unto his pieces, and unto his head.*

God gave further instructions to cut and wash the pieces of the ram and his head. Just like Jesus is the head of the church, when

93

we are broken, cut, bruised or going through something, we can lay at the feet of Jesus.

Exodus 29:18, 19 *And thou shalt burn the whole ram upon the altar: it is a burnt offering unto the Lord: it is a sweet savour, an offering made by fire unto the Lord. And thou shalt take the other ram; and Aaron and his sons shall put their hands upon the head of the ram.*

Aaron and his sons were instructed to burn the whole ram on the altar so that it would be a sweet savor unto the Lord. They also put their hands upon the head of the rams. This reminds me of how the five-fold ministry (apostles, prophets, evangelists, pastors and teachers) is supposed to delegate and show the saints how to carry out the will of God according to Ephesians 4:11, 12.

Exodus 29:20 *Then shalt thou kill the ram, and take of his blood, and put it upon the tip of the right ear of Aaron, and upon the tip of the right ear of his sons, and upon the thumb of their right hand, and upon the great toe of their right foot, and sprinkle the blood upon the altar round about.*

Once the ram was killed, its blood had to be applied to certain areas and on certain people. Because Aaron and his sons were priests, they placed the blood on their right ears (to hear God right), on their right thumb (everything they put their hands to would prosper), and to their big right toe (to walk in the path of righteousness).They sprinkled the blood on the altar because they executed the sprinkling of blood around the altar seven times.

Exodus 29:21 *And thou shalt take of the blood that is upon the altar, and of the anointing oil, and sprinkle it upon Aaron, and upon his garments, and upon his sons, and upon the garments of his sons with him: and he shall be hallowed, and his garments, and his sons, and his sons' garments with him.*

The blood was to be sprinkled on Aaron's and his sons' garments with the anointing oil so that he, his sons and their garments would be hallowed. I remember hearing a teaching on the blood and the anointing and the man of God said that we should plead the blood over our family members' clothes as we wash them and I agree with that. We also need to pray and plead the blood over the clothes we purchase and also over the hotel rooms we enter.

Leviticus 1:5 *And he shall kill the bullock before the Lord: and the priests, Aaron's sons, shall bring the blood, and sprinkle the blood round about upon the altar that is by the door of the tabernacle of the congregation.*

Aaron's sons were to bring the blood around the altar by the door of the tabernacle of the congregation so that the whole congregation could be cleaned by the blood.

Leviticus 1:11 *And he shall kill it on the side of the altar northward before the Lord: and the priests, Aaron's sons, shall sprinkle his blood round about upon the altar.*

In the Old Testament, the priests had to sprinkle the blood at the altar. There is something about bringing things to the altar and leaving them there. Surely the Lord's presence meets us at the altar of prayer and anywhere else we call upon His name.

Here is a list of more scriptures about sprinkling the blood:

Leviticus 3:8– *And he shall lay his hand upon the head of his offering, and kill it before the tabernacle of the congregation:*

and Aaron's sons shall sprinkle the blood thereof round about upon the altar.

Leviticus 3:13– *And he shall lay his hand upon the head of it, and kill it before the tabernacle of the congregation: and the sons of Aaron shall sprinkle the blood thereof upon the altar round about.*

Leviticus 4:6–*And the priest shall dip his finger in the blood, and sprinkle of the blood seven times before the Lord, before the vail of the sanctuary.*

Sprinkling the blood seven times was very important. Before I preached at a conference that the Lord led me to have, He told me to plead the blood seven times before I preached. I obeyed God and that day we raised about $1,300.00 from less than 50 people. If God's people sprinkled the blood seven times, I figured I can do the same thing.

Leviticus 4:16-18– *And the priest that is anointed shall bring of the bullock's blood to the tabernacle of the congregation: And the priest shall dip his finger in some of the blood, and sprinkle it <u>seven times</u> before the Lord, even before the vail. And he shall put some of the blood upon the horns of the altar which is before the Lord that is in the tabernacle of the congregation, and shall pour out all the blood at the bottom of the altar of the burnt offering, which is at the door of the tabernacle of the congregation.*

Here again we see the priests sprinkle the blood seven times before the Lord; just like Moses sprinkled the ashes before Pharaoh, and a MIRACLE took place.

Leviticus 5:9– *And he shall sprinkle of the blood of the sin offering upon the side of the altar; and the rest of the blood shall be wrung out at the bottom of the altar: it is a sin offering.*

Honor the blood over the sins in your life that you know you need to be delivered from.

Leviticus 7:2– *In the place where they kill the burnt offering shall they kill the trespass offering: and the blood thereof shall he sprinkle round about upon the altar.*

All of us have our own personal altars; the place where we present our sacrifices unto the Lord. SPRINKLE THE BLOOD WHEREVER YOUR ALTAR IS.

Leviticus 14:7– *And he shall sprinkle upon him that is to be cleansed from the leprosy seven times, and shall pronounce him clean, and shall let the living bird loose into the open field.*

Leprosy was considered a form of disease in the Old Testament and individuals with the disease were restricted from the public. For a leper to be cleansed, the priest had to kill a bird and sprinkle its blood on the leper seven times. Then the priest would pronounce him cleansed and let the second living bird loose into the field.

This scripture found in **Leviticus 14:16-18** refers to the process the leper and the priest went through in order for the leper to be cleansed. Instead of blood, the priest sprinkled the soil seven times before the Lord and anoints the tip of the leper's right ear, right thumb, and the great toe of his right foot.

Leviticus 14:27-29 – *And the priest shall sprinkle with his right finger some of the oil that is in his left hand seven times*

97

before the Lord: And the priest shall put of the oil that is in his hand upon the tip of the right ear of him that is to be cleansed, and upon the thumb of his right hand, and upon the great toe of his right foot, upon the place of the blood of the trespass offering: And the rest of the oil that is in the priest's hand he shall put upon the head of him that is to be cleansed, to make atonement for him before the Lord.

Leviticus 14:51-53 *– And he shall take the cedar wood, and the hyssop, and the scarlet, and the living bird, and dip them in the blood of the slain bird, and in the running water, and sprinkle the house seven times: And he shall cleanse the house with the blood of the bird, and with the running water, and with the living bird, and with the cedar wood, and with the hyssop, and with the scarlet: But he shall let go the living bird out of the city into the open fields, and make an atonement for the house: and it shall be clean.*

To clean a house of a plague the house must be shut up for seven days. On the seventh day, the priest would inspect the house of the plague. If the house was still unclean to the priest, they would sprinkle the blood on the house seven times for a cleansing.

Leviticus 16:14,15– *And he shall take of the blood of the bullock, and sprinkle it with his finger upon the mercy seat eastward; and before the mercy seat shall he sprinkle of the blood with his finger seven times. Then shall he kill the goat of the sin offering that is for the people and bring his blood within the vail, and do with that blood as he did with the blood of the bullock, and sprinkle it upon the mercy seat, and before the mercy seat:*

Sprinkle the blood before the mercy seat of heaven where the doors are always open. Plead the blood from the mercy seat upon things in your life that must change.

Leviticus 16:17-19– *And there shall be no man in the tabernacle of the congregation when he goeth into make an atonement in the holy place, until he come out, and have made an atonement for himself, and for his household, and for all the congregation of Israel. And he shall go out unto the altar that is before the Lord, and make atonement for it; and shall take of the blood of the bullock, and of the blood of the goat, and put it upon the horns of the altar round about. And he shall sprinkle of the blood upon it with his finger seven times, and cleanse it, and hallow it from the uncleanness of the children of Israel.*

There are two things to remember about this verse:
1. The blood was sprinkled seven times on the behalf of the priest, his household and his entire congregation.
2. The purpose of sprinkling the blood seven times was to cleanse and hallow.

I have noticed that whenever I say the blood seven times at any time a change happens in whatever I am speaking to. The priests had to sprinkle the blood seven times. Seven is a powerful number.

On the seventh day, God rested after creating the world.

Leviticus 17:6– *And the priest shall sprinkle the blood upon the altar of the Lord at the door of the tabernacle of the congregation, and burn the fat for a sweet savour unto the Lord.*

Honoring the blood as we enter the presence of the Lord is essential because we have a blood-bought right to receive answers to our prayers in Jesus' name.

Numbers 8:7– *And thus shalt thou do unto them, to cleanse them (the Levities): Sprinkle water of purifying upon them, and let them shave all their flesh, and let them wash their clothes, and so make themselves clean.*

Numbers 18:17–*But the firstling of a cow, or the firstling of a sheep, or the firstling of a goat, thou shalt not redeem; they are holy: thou shalt sprinkle their blood upon the altar, and shalt burn their fat for an offering made by fire, for a sweet savor unto the Lord.*

Numbers 19:4-6; 18-19– *And Eleazar the priest shall take of her (the red heifer) blood with his finger, and sprinkle of her blood directly before the tabernacle of the congregation seven times: And one shall burn the heifer in his sight; her skin, and her flesh, and her blood, with her dung, shall he burn: And the priest shall take cedar wood, and hyssop, and scarlet, and cast it into the midst of the burning of the heifer.[18]And a clean person shall take hyssop, and dip it in the water, and sprinkle it upon the tent, and upon all the vessels, and upon the persons that were there, and upon him that touched a bone, or one slain, or one dead, or a grave: And the clean person shall sprinkle upon the unclean on the third day, and on the seventh day: and on the seventh day he shall purify himself, and wash his clothes, and bathe himself in water, and shall be clean at even.*

2 Kings 16:15– *And king Ahaz commanded Uriah the priest, saying, Upon the great altar burn the morning burnt offering,* *and the evening meat offering, and the king's burnt sacrifice, and meat offering, with the burnt offering of all the people of the land, and their meat offering, and their drink offerings; and sprinkle upon it all the blood of the burnt offering, and all the blood of the sacrifice: and the brazen altar shall be for me to inquire by.*

Isaiah 52:15– *So shall he (Jesus) sprinkle many nations; the kings shall shut their mouths at him: for that which had not been told them shall they see; and that which they had not heard shall they consider.*

Ezekiel 36:25– *Then will I sprinkle clean water upon you, and ye shall be clean: from all your filthiness, and from all your idols, will I cleanse you.*

Ezekiel 43:18– *And he said unto me, Son of man, thus saith the Lord God; These are the ordinances of the altar in the day when they shall make it, to offer burnt offerings thereon, and to sprinkle blood thereon.*

All these scriptures refer to sprinkling the blood, ashes, and water for things to happen. When the Lord leads you to meditate upon the sprinkling of the blood in the Bible; people and all the vessels of the ministry, according to Hebrews 9:17-22, something great will happen. When I go to the house of God, hear the Word of God, and want to seal that word in my heart; I take the blood (communion) over the word just like Moses and the children of Israel did. The precepts were read for us to do them.

101

Here are more scripture references for the words sprinkled, sprinkling and sprinkleth.

Sprinkled

Exodus 9:10 – *And they took ashes of the furnace, and stood before Pharaoh: and Moses sprinkled it (the ashes) up toward heaven; and it became a boil breaking forth with blains upon man, and upon beast.*

Exodus 24:6-8– *And Moses took half of the blood, and put it in basins; and half of the blood he sprinkled on the altar. And he took the book of the covenant, and read in the audience of the people: and they said, All that the Lord hath said will we do, and be obedient. And Moses took the blood, and sprinkled it on the people, and said, Behold the blood of the covenant, which the Lord hath made with you concerning all these words.*

Moses sealed the words that the people spoke when applying the blood. They had a binding contract with the covenant of the words that Moses read from the Word of God.

Leviticus 6:26, 27 –*The priest that offereth it for sin shall eat it: in the holy place shall it be eaten, in the court of the tabernacle of the congregation. Whatsoever shall touch the flesh thereof shall be holy: and when there is sprinkled of the blood thereof upon any garment, thou shalt wash that whereon it was sprinkled in the holy place.*

Leviticus 8:10, 11– *And Moses took the anointing oil, and anointed the tabernacle and all that was therein, and sanctified them. And he sprinkled thereof upon the altar seven times, and anointed the altar and all his vessels, both the laver and his foot, to sanctify them.*

Remember the number seven is the number of completion.

Leviticus 8:19 – *And he (Aaron) killed it; and Moses sprinkled the blood upon the altar round about.*

Leviticus 8:23, 24–*And he (Moses) slew it (the other ram); and Moses took of the blood of it, and put it upon the tip of Aaron's right ear, and upon the thumb of his right hand, and upon the great toe of his right foot. And he brought Aaron's sons, and Moses put of the blood upon the tip of their right ear, and upon the thumbs of their right hands, and upon the great toes of their right feet: and Moses sprinkled the blood upon the altar round about.*

Leviticus 8:30 – *And Moses took of the anointing oil, and of the blood which was upon the altar, and sprinkled it upon Aaron, and upon his garments, and upon his sons, and upon his sons' garments with him; and sanctified Aaron, and his garments, and his sons, and his sons' garments with him.*

Leviticus 9:8-12– *Aaron therefore went unto the altar, and slew the calf of the sin offering, which was for himself. And the sons of Aaron brought the blood unto him: and he dipped his finger in the blood, and put it upon the horns of the altar, and poured out the blood at the bottom of the altar: But the fat, and the kidneys, and the caul above the liver of the sin offering, he burnt upon the altar; as the Lord commanded Moses. And the flesh and the hide he burnt with fire without the camp. And he slew the burnt offering; and Aaron's sons presented unto him the blood, which he sprinkled round about upon the altar.*

Aaron also slew the bullock and the ram for a sacrifice of peace offerings for the people and his sons. The blood was presented to him, which he sprinkled upon the altar.

Numbers 19:13,20– *Whosoever toucheth the dead body of any man that is dead, and purifieth not himself, defileth the tabernacle of the Lord; and that soul shall be cut off from Israel:*

because the water of separation was not sprinkled upon him, he shall be unclean; his uncleanness is yet upon him. [20] *But the man that shall be unclean, and shall not purify himself, that soul shall be cut off from among the congregation, because he hath defiled the sanctuary of the Lord: the water of separation hath not been sprinkled upon him; he is unclean.*

2 Kings 9:33– *And he said, throw her down. So they threw her down: and some of her blood was sprinkled on the wall, and on the horses: and he trode her under foot.* (This verse refers to Jezebel when she is thrown from a window and later eaten by dogs).

2 Kings 16:13– *And he (King Ahaz) burnt his burnt offering and his meat offering, and poured his drink offering, and sprinkled the blood of his peace offerings, upon the altar.*

2 Chronicles 29:22– *So they killed the bullocks, and the priests received the blood, and sprinkled it on the altar: likewise, when they had killed the rams, they sprinkled the blood upon the altar: they killed also the lambs, and they sprinkled the blood upon the altar.*

2 Chronicles 30:15, 16 – *Then they killed the Passover on the fourteenth day of the second month: and the priests and the Levites were ashamed, and sanctified themselves, and brought in the burnt offerings into the house of the Lord. And they stood in their place after their manner, according to the law of Moses the man of God: the priests sprinkled the blood, which they received of the hand of the Levites.*

2 Chronicles 35:11– *And they killed the passover, and the priests sprinkled the blood from their hands, and the Levites flayed them.*

Job 2:12– *And when they lifted up their eyes afar off, and knew him not, they lifted up their voice, and wept; and they rent* *everyone his mantle, and sprinkled dust upon their heads toward heaven.*

Isaiah 63:3, 4– *I have trodden the winepress alone; and of the people there was none with me: for I will tread them in mine anger, and trample them in my fury; and their blood shall be sprinkled upon my garments, and I will stain all my raiment. For the day of vengeance is in mine heart, and the year of my redeemed is come.*

Hebrews 9:18-22 – *Whereupon neither the first testament was dedicated without blood. For when Moses had spoken every precept to all the people according to the law, he took the blood of calves and of goats, with water, and scarlet wool, and hyssop, and sprinkled both the book, and all the people, Saying, This is the blood of the testament which God hath enjoined unto you. Moreover he (Moses) sprinkled with blood both the tabernacle, and all the vessels of the ministry. And almost all things are by the law purged with blood; and without shedding of blood is no remission.*

Hebrews 10:22– *Let us draw near with a true heart in full assurance of faith, having our hearts sprinkled from an evil conscience, and our bodies washed with pure water.*

Sprinkleth

Leviticus 7:14– *And of it he shall offer one out of the whole oblation for an heave offering unto the Lord, and it shall be the priest's that sprinkleth the blood of the peace offerings.*

Number 19:21– *And it shall be a perpetual statute unto them, that he that sprinkleth the water of separation shall wash* *his clothes; and he that toucheth the water of separation shall be unclean until even.*

Sprinkling

Hebrews 9:13-15– *For if the blood of bulls and of goats, and the ashes of an heifer sprinkling the unclean, sanctifieth to the purifying of the flesh: How much more shall the blood of Christ, who through the eternal Spirit offered himself without spot to God, purge your conscience from dead works to serve the living God? And for this cause he is the mediator of the New Testament that by means of death, for the redemption of the transgressions that were under the first testament, they which are called might receive the promise of eternal inheritance.*

Hebrews 11:28– *Through faith he (Moses) kept the passover, and the sprinkling of blood, lest he that destroyed the firstborn should touch them.*

Hebrews 12:24– *And to Jesus the mediator of the new covenant, and to the blood of sprinkling, that speaketh better things than that of Abel.*

I Peter 1:2– *Elect according to the foreknowledge of God the Father, through sanctification of the Spirit, unto obedience and sprinkling of the blood of Jesus Christ: Grace unto you, and peace, be multiplied.*

The scriptures in the Old Testament concerning the blood being sprinkled seven times means: what they offered up before God on the altar was finished. Just as Jesus said the words "IT IS FINISHED"; those words contain 12 letters, and the number 12 means government. The government is established on His shoulders. Everything can be governed by our words when we honor the blood by sprinkling it over situations in Jesus name.

Chapter Twenty
Victory over Satan through the Blood

How do we as Christians receive victory over Satan through the blood? This is done by putting our faith in the blood of Jesus and the power of His death, burial and resurrection.

Revelation 12:11 says, "And they overcame him (Satan) by the blood of the Lamb, and by the word of their testimony; and they loved not their lives unto the death."

There is a greater power on the inside of us through Jesus Christ. The scripture didn't say we *overcome* Satan, but we *overcame* Satan by the blood of the Lamb (Jesus Christ) who defeated him "according as he hath chosen us in him before the foundation of the world, that we should be holy and without blame before him in love:" (Ephesians 1:4). Since we were chosen by God before the foundation of the world, Satan has already been defeated by the blood of the Lamb. Remember, God calleth those things that be not as though they were.

Jesus is our brethren, our high priest, the apostle of our soul. We stand in the victory of what the Word of God says. The blood of the Lamb causes us to overcome.

André Crouch wrote a song when he was about thirteen and it was later placed in the Baptist hymnal. The song is about the blood. One verse is this:

The blood that Jesus shed for me way back on Calvary

The blood that gives me strength from day to day, it will never lose its power.

Let's look at I John 5:4-8:"For whatsoever is born of God overcometh the world: and this is the victory that overcometh the world, even our faith" (1 John 5:4).

We the believers are born of God. We overcome the world through faith and the Word of God the Father.

Verse *[5]Who is he that overcometh the world, but he that believeth that Jesus is the son of God?* We only overcome the world once we believe that Jesus is the son of God and we receive Him into our lives.

> *[6]This is he that came by water and blood, even Jesus Christ; not by water only, but by water and blood. And it is the Spirit that beareth witness, because the spirit is truth.*

Three elements are mentioned in verse 6: water, blood and spirit. This three-fold cord that symbolizes the Trinity (Father, Son and the Holy Ghost) cannot be broken. The spirit beareth witness because it is truth.

> *[7]For there are three that beareth record in heaven, the Father, the Word, and the Holy Ghost: and these three are one.*

Another three-fold cord is the Father, the Son, and the Holy Spirit in heaven. All three are one and agree on everything. They are not becoming one but they are one.

> *[8]And there are three that bear witness in earth, the Spirit, and the water, and the blood: and these three agree in one.*

The Spirit, water and the blood are another three-fold cord. Together they are manifest; because, there is an agreement in the earth whenever the three are mentioned.

Take note that the Holy Spirit and the blood are the last two anointing mentioned at the end of the three-fold. I have seen that whenever the blood is preached, sang or taught, the Holy Spirit is released in the atmosphere and elevates its recipients to a higher dimension.

In 2006, my husband and I dealt with witchcraft and God gave us the victory through the blood. I remembered that the blood worked on the doors in Egypt when they applied it; so, it will certainly work against witches and warlocks. We honored communion morning and evening over the spirit in that person. We still honor it because Jesus said to remember Him in the communion cup. Anything we need victory in we need to know that Jesus already overcame Satan by the blood. All we need to do is live in the fullness of God.

> *And I saw as it were a sea of glass mingled with fire: and them that had gotten the victory over the beast, and over his image, and over his mark, and over the number of his name, stand on the sea of glass, having the harps of God. And they sing the song of Moses the servant of God, and the song of the Lamb, saying, Great and marvelous are thy works, Lord God Almighty; just and true are thy ways, thou King of saints* (Revelation 15: 2, 3).

John, the author of the Book of Revelation, saw in a vision that the victory was won over the beast, his image, his mark, and the number of his name. God saw the victory over Satan ahead of time. We should also see the victory over Satan ahead of time. After seeing the victory over Satan, they sang the songs of Moses.

When we want to see the character of the Lord God Almighty, this verse shows us that God is ***VICTORIOUS.***

I want to share a poem that I wrote:

109

Moses the servant of God knew when to depart
Came out of Egypt with the blood on the door
When they came out they were not poor
Came out as one
Because they knew the miracle was done
The purpose in them coming out was to worship God
But, as they went alone they made things hard
They were guided by a cloud of a pillar by night
Therefore, they had to depend on the light
When they needed water for provision it came forth
So, they could continue on to the vision
We have favor and we know the savior
We are born of God; therefore, He doesn't make things hard
We are blessed with all spiritual blessings, so we can learn
God's lessons (the Word)

I pray that something was said or written to enlighten you and to enhance the growth that is needed in your life. If you have not accepted Jesus Christ as your Lord and Savior, I would like to invite you to come into the kingdom of God by repeating this prayer:

> Father God, I recognize and admit that I am a sinner according to Psalms 51:5, for *I was shapen in iniquity; and in sin did my mother conceive me*. Romans 10:9, 10 says "That if thou shalt confess with thy mouth the Lord Jesus, and shalt believe in thine heart that God hath raised him (Jesus) from the dead, thou shalt be saved. For with the heart man believeth unto righteousness; and with the mouth confession is made unto salvation. "Therefore I confess with my mouth the Lord Jesus and I believe in my heart that God raised Him from the dead, and I

am saved through the confession of my mouth in Jesus' name.

Whatever the need is in your life, the Word of God is the answer. Find the scriptures that meet your need, honor the communion over them, believe God, and watch miracles happen.
We often see signs that say "COMING SOON." With the help of the Holy Spirit another book will be coming soon in Jesus name!!!!!!!

Chapter Twenty-One
12 Reasons Why We Should Take Communion at Home

There are more than 12 reasons why we should take communion in our homes; but, the number 12 carries it weight of importance in scriptures:

1. Jesus chose 12 apostles (Matthew 10:2-4)
2. Jesus was 12 years old when He was in the temple confounding the religious leaders(Luke 2:42)
3. There are 12 gates to the city of Heaven (3 in the north, south, east and west(Revelation 21:13)
4. There are 12 Tribes of Israel(Revelation 7:4-8)
5. Jesus took up 12 baskets of leftovers at an occasion (John 6:12,13)
6. 12 months in a year (January- December)
7. 12 apostles of the Lamb (Revelation 21:14)
8. 12 foundations in the wall of the city (Revelation 21:14)
9. 12 gates with 12 pearls (Revelation 21:21)
10. 12 precious stones (Revelation 21:19, 20)
11. Jesus could have called 12 legions of angels when He was crucified to take His place (Matthew 26:53)
12. 12 lions in Solomon's kingdom (I Kings 10:20)

Here are twelve reasons along with explanations and biblical examples of why we should honor communion (the Blood) in our homes.

Reason 1: God said the blood is a token (sign) on our

house

And the blood shall be to you for a token upon the houses where ye are: and when I see the blood, I will pass over you, and the plague shall not be upon you to destroy you, when I smite the land of Egypt (Exodus 12:13).

Read Exodus 12:7-13, Luke 22:7-14 and Acts 2:41-47.

Our house is where we live. We place our focus on things inside our homes; whether, it is our spiritual homes, family or church home. Acts 1:8 says, "...ye shall be witnesses unto me both in Jerusalem, and in all Judea, and in Samaria, and unto the uttermost part of the earth."
God said the blood must be upon the houses. It isn't enough just to know about the blood, we must honor the blood in our lives and homes. What good would it have done if the Israelites left the blood in the basin and did not apply it to the door and side posts of their houses? Applying the blood to your home turns away all manner of evil that may try to enter in and brings in the power of God to move on our behalf. In Genesis 3, God had to put animal blood on Adam and Eve after they committed the first sin against His command (Genesis 3:21). The blood was not needed until SIN showed up.
When we obey the road and traffic signs and laws, we receive a form of victory. We don't get any tickets, have a good driving record and lower our insurance rates. The same should be applied when we obey God's Word: victory is inevitable.

In Luke 22, Jesus had the apostles (sent ones) go and prepare the Passover supper in the Upper Room. The Upper Room was a form of a house where the commandment of communion was honored. The Book of Acts shows us that people went from house to house "breaking bread" and fellowshipping. The bread symbolizes the body of Jesus Christ, a major part of communion. The passage in Exodus 12 talks about when God commanded the people of Israel to take the blood and strike it on the two side posts and on the upper door post of their houses, and to eat all of it afterwards.

Why did God instruct them to use blood? Why not mud or something else? The blood was a sign of Jesus the Lamb that would shed His blood for the whole world. Once the blood was put on the houses, nothing could come in to destroy them. We know the blood will never lose its power. The blood will protect the house of those who honor the blood inside their homes.

When we accepted Jesus Christ into our heart, the blood cleansed the sins that had us in darkness and made us white as snow. It commanded death to pass over us! HALLELUJAH!

***Reason 2:* God commanded that the Lord's Passover be taught through the generations (Exodus 12:24-28).**

My personal reason for honoring communion every day is found in I Corinthians 11:23-26. Jesus asked us to remember Him for what He did for us in shedding His blood, rising on the third day, and sitting at the right hand of the Father interceding for His body (Christians). Jesus says:

Remember my body was broken for you.
Remember my blood was shed for you. REMEMBER THAT.

Every day when I spend time with God in prayer and read the Word, I make a decision to remember the words of Jesus about the BLOOD!

And ye shall observe this thing for an ordinance to thee and to the sons forever (Exodus 12:24).

The people of God were commanded to observe the Passover; not once a month or once a year but forever. They celebrated for 7 days during the Passover in this chapter.

Verse [25] *And it shall come to pass, when ye be come to the land which the Lord will give you, according as he hath promised, that ye shall keep this service.*

This is the second time the Lord told the Israelites to keep the service of the Passover. They were going to a new land and God wanted them to understand that they must continue to execute the Passover even in a new place. God gave them land which He promised them but they had to sanctify the land with the blood. Whatever is on the land that doesn't belong will have to die.

[26-27]*And it shall come to pass, when your children shall say unto you, What mean ye by this service? That ye shall say, It is the sacrifice of the Lord's passover who passed over the houses of the children of Israel in Egypt, when he smote the Egyptians, and delivered our houses. And the people bowed the head and worshipped*

Children are full of questions, so the Lord instructed the children of Israel to continue to honor the Passover. Whenever the children ask why, they are told "It is the sacrifice of the Lord's Passover who passed over the houses of the children of Israel when the death angel came through." It was and still is important for children to know that the blood is the protecting agent.

[28] *And the children of Israel went away, and did as the Lord had commanded Moses and Aaron, so did they.*

The Lord said that the service of the Lord's Passover was to be kept when they got into the land that He promised them. Because God brought them from one land to the Promised Land, it was an occasion to be celebrated.

After the same manner also he took the cup, when he had supped, saying, This cup is the new testament in my blood: this do ye, as oft as ye drink it, in remembrance of me. For as often as ye eat this bread, and drink this cup, ye do shew the Lord's death till he come (I Corinthians 11:25, 26).

We are to honor the Lord's Passover in the New Testament like the Old Testament.
It is the blood that sets us free from sin.
It is the blood that makes us white as snow.
It is the blood that brought us from hell to heaven.
It is the blood that causes the death angel to pass over our houses.

Reason 3: _The blood causes the death angel, the plague and the destroyer to passover our families_

For I will pass through the land of Egypt this night, and will smite all the firstborn in the land of Egypt, both man and beast; and against all the gods of Egypt I will execute judgment: I am the Lord. And the blood shall be to you for a token upon the houses where ye are: and when I see the blood, I will passover you, and the plague shall not be upon you to destroy you, when I smite the land of Egypt (Exodus 12:12, 13).

In verse 12, God told the children of Israel that He was going to send a death angel to pass through the land during the night to destroy every firstborn. The land of the Egyptians represents the world system and when God sent the death angel to the land. He killed everything that did not honor the blood. The blood from the sacrifices protected every man and their family from the death angel. If we honor the blood in our lives, the blood will always protect us. God destroyed the false gods because He doesn't want anything before Him. Likewise, He will look at our lives to see if the blood of Jesus is honored. When He sees the blood, He will not execute judgment upon us.

The blood is a token or a sign to pay attention to and should be applied to our houses and lives. When God sees the blood on your houses(in your heart), He will cause the death angel to pass over you. It will not come near your dwelling (you) neither will the plague (sickness and diseases) be upon you to destroy you. God will even prevent the plague from being on our bodies. Exodus 15:26 says, "…If thou (Israel) wilt diligently hearken to the voice of the Lord thy God, and wilt do that which is right in his sight, and wilt give ear to his commandments, and keep all his statutes, I will put none of these diseases upon thee, which I have brought upon the Egyptians: for I am the Lord that healeth thee."
God said that He would not put the same diseases on the Israelites that He put on the Egyptians because they obeyed His commandments.

Exodus 23:25 says, "And ye shall serve the Lord your God, and he shall bless thy bread, and thy water; and I will take sickness away from the midst of thee." God promised that He would take sickness away from those who obey His commandments.
The blood of Jesus was shed to bring healing to our bodies according to I Peter 2:24 which said "Who his own self bare our sins in his own body on the tree, that we, being dead to sins, should live unto righteousness: by whose stripes ye were

healed." By the stripes of Jesus the Lamb, we were already healed; therefore, we are healed.

Reason 4: Honoring communion prevents the destroyer from entering our houses and overtaking us

For the Lord will pass through to smite the Egyptians; and when he seeth the blood upon the lintel, and on the two side posts, the Lord will passover the door, and will not suffer the destroyer to come in unto your houses Exodus 12:23,24).

The Word of the Lord said He would pass through to smite the Egyptians (world system); but, when He saw the blood upon the houses, the Lord passed over. The Word says that the Lord "will", not "might", pass over the house that is covered with the blood.

The Israelites had to choose a flawless lamb and kill it for the Passover. The blood of the lamb was already there for protection before they killed it and smeared its blood on their door and side posts.

Jesus was the Lamb of God that was slain for our protection. When we put His blood on our lives, just as the children of Israel put the blood on their door frames, the destroyer will pass over us, just as it passed over the children of Israel. God was and is looking for the blood.

The Israelites had to put the blood on the doors in the shape of a cross on the side posts and the lintel to keep the destroyer from coming pass the bloodline. What are some of the "destroyers" that are trying to come into the home? Remember, they cannot come in because the Word of God says the blood will not suffer (permit) the destroyer to come into our houses to smite us. Just as the destroyer was not permitted and did not smite the Israelites, the same applies to us (the believers). We are the seed of Abraham. Satan could not touch Job because God had a hedge around him. The blood is a hedge of protection around us.

"Destroyers"

- Sin
- Satan
- Sickness
- Poverty
- Pride
- Lust

- Laziness
- Fear
- Failure
- Marital Situations
- Money
- etc.

Verse 24 is the key to the destroyer not coming to smite us. We shall observe to keep the Lord's Passover just as He commanded Israel to observe and keep the Passover in their houses.

Reason 5: The Blood brings deliverance

That ye shall say, It is the sacrifice of the Lord's Passover, who passed over the houses of the children of Israel in Egypt, when he smote the Egyptians, and delivered our houses. And the people bowed the head and worshipped. (Exodus 12:27-29)

119

When we need deliverance, we should honor the blood in our houses. It is the sacrifice of the Lord's Passover who passed over the houses of the children of Israel (light). When God returns, He will be looking for a church that has His Son's blood on their lives. Once God delivered the houses covered by the blood ,the people bowed their heads and worshipped. When we are delivered from evil, we should worship the Father God.

Verse [28:] *And the children of Israel went away, and did as the Lord had commanded Moses and Aaron, so do they.*
Remember, the Egyptians had no blood on their houses; so, they had no life and no reason to be protected from the death angel. The blood kept the Israelites alive because they followed the instruction of their leaders Moses and Aaron.

[29:]*And it came to pass, that at midnight the Lord smote all the firstborn in the land of Egypt, from the firstborn of Pharaoh that sat on his throne unto the firstborn of the captive that was in the dungeon; and all the firstborn of cattle.*

At midnight, the Lord killed those who did not follow His word (instruction). In Acts 16:25, 26 the Word says: "…at midnight Paul and Silas prayed, and sang praises unto God: and the prisoners heard them. And suddenly there was a great earthquake, so that the foundations of the prison were shaken: and immediately all the doors were opened and every one's bands were loosed. "Something happened during Paul and Silas' midnight prayer meeting. Not only did God hear them, but the prisoners heard them and saw the power of prayer and praise.
The prayer and singing caused a great earthquake and immediately all the doors were opened. Everyone was free.

Other scriptures of things that took place at midnight:

- Judges 16:3 – Samson takes the gates of the city off at midnight.
- Ruth 3:8 – Ruth lies at the feet of Boaz at midnight.
- I Kings 3:20 – The children's switch occurred at midnight.
- Psalm 119:62 – David rose at midnight to give thanks.
- Matthew 25:6 – The "midnight cry" of the bridegroom's arrival to the 10 virgins.
- Mark 13:35 – The scenario of the Son of man's arrival may occur at midnight.
- Luke 11:5 – The knock of a friend for three loaves at midnight.
- Acts 20:7 – Apostle Paul preached until midnight.
- Acts 27:27 – Apostle Paul and other men travelled at midnight.

From the scriptures above, we know that there is significance when things happen at midnight. Sometimes my husband and I will take communion at midnight for a specific thing. The power of the blood protected the Israelites at midnight also. To God, it didn't matter who didn't have the blood on their houses, the instruction had to be followed to guarantee survival from the death angel.

Colossians 1:13, 14 say, "Who hath delivered us from the power of darkness, and hath translated us into the kingdom of his dear son: In whom we have redemption through his blood, even the forgiveness of sins: "We have already been delivered from the power of darkness through the redemption of the shed blood of Jesus Christ. We have been translated into the kingdom of God's dear son Jesus.

Ephesians 1:7 says, "In whom we have redemption through his blood, the forgiveness of sins, according to the riches of His grace: "We have redemption and the forgiveness of our sins through Christ's blood.

Reason 6: *The Blood takes away the sin of the world.*

The next day John seeth Jesus coming unto him, and saith, Behold the Lamb of God, which taketh away the sin of the world (John 1:29).

John the Baptist announced the Lamb of God's arrival. He said "behold" or "look "and used the term "Lamb of God", because lambs in Exodus were slain to put the blood on the doors in Goshen. Just as the blood took away sins back then, the blood will take away sins now. The Lamb of God is not adding sins to our lives; but, is taking them away through the blood and the Word of God. The blood of Jesus Christ is guaranteed power to make us white as snow.

I remember when I gave my life to Jesus on January 16, 1977. The weight of my sins was lifted off of me. Even though I don't go by feeling, I felt so light that night because my life had changed forever.

And as they were eating, Jesus took bread, and blessed it, and brake it, and gave it to the disciples, and said, Take, eat; this is my body. And he took the cup, and gave thanks, and gave it to them, saying, Drink ye all of it. For this is my blood of the new testament, which is shed for many for the remission of sins

(Matthew 26:26-28) Jesus and his disciples were sitting at a meal when Jesus took the bread and did four things:
1. Blessed it
2. Brake it
3. Gave it
4. Said eat it

I like receiving the bread of life from Jesus Christ, the Son and I bless the Heavenly Father forgiving the Word to us. The Word breaks situations in our lives and we need to give the

Word to others by telling them to take, eat, and meditate on God's Word.

When Jesus took the cup in verse 27, He gave thanks, gave to others and gave an instruction to drink all of "it"; referring to the fruit of the vine. In others words, He said to drink the "full", not "partial", benefits of me. Drink the fullness of Christ.

Drinking from the cup lets us know that the blood seals the covenant that Jesus shed to remit our sins. We no longer have to live in sin because the blood has paid the ransom for sin. Jesus established the blood as a New Testament doctrine.

And he said unto them, This is my blood of the new testament, which is shed for many (Mark 14:24).In verses 22 and 23 Jesus blessed the bread and gave to them showing us how to give thanks because His body was given for us. The blood of Jesus was shed to establish the New Testament so that many can be saved.

And he took bread, and gave thanks, and brake it, and gave unto them, saying, This is my body which is given for you: this do in remembrance of me. Likewise also the cup after supper, saying, This cup is the new testament in my blood, which is shed for you (Luke 22:19, 20).

Here are seven points in Luke's account of the Last Supper:
1. Jesus took the bread
2. He gave thanks
3. He brake the bread
4. He gave to the disciples
5. He said "This is my body that I am giving for you"
6. He took the cup after the supper meal

7. He let it be known that this cup is the New Testament and my blood was shed for you. The "you" in Luke's account referred to the Apostles.

Being justified freely by his grace through the redemption that is in Christ Jesus: Whom God hath set forth to be a propitiation through faith in his blood, to declare his righteousness for the remission of sins that are past, through the forbearance of God (Romans 3:24, 25).We are justified freely by God's grace. The word "justified "here means that we are just like Jesus as though we never sinned. In other words, we have the righteousness of Jesus Christ, the Redeemer, who brought us back from one hand (Satan) to another (God). Jesus Christ rescued us from the hand of the enemy (Satan).

God sent Jesus Christ to be the sacrificial Lamb for the sins of the world. Therefore, we put our trust and faith in the blood that was shed so that we can declare His righteousness. The blood has remitted our sins. The blood gave us a right to be free from sin making us the righteousness of God in Christ Jesus.

Here is a confession of faith in the blood: THROUGH FAITH IN THE BLOOD I HAVE BEEN SET FREE FROM SIN AND I CAN DECLARE GOD'S RIGHTEOUSNESS INTO MY LIFE. GOD HATH SET IT FORTH IN CHRIST JESUS.

Hebrews 9:18 says: Whereupon neither the first testament was dedicated without blood. [19]For when Moses had spoken every precept to all the people according to the law, he took the blood of calves and of goats, with water, scarlet wool, and hyssop, and sprinkled both the book, and all the people. [20]Saying, "This is the blood of the testament which God hath enjoined unto you". [21]Moreover, He sprinkled with blood both the tabernacle, and all the vessels of the ministry. [22]And almost all things are by the law purged with blood; and without the shedding of blood, is no remission. (KJV)

Verse 18 tells us that the Old Testament was dedicated with the blood. Moses spoke every precept God gave him to all the people. After he spoke the precepts, he took the blood and sprinkled both the book (the Word of God) and all the people. He sealed the words he spoke to the people with the blood of calves and goats so that no precept would depart from their hearts. This would also join them to the Word of God. Then Moses sprinkled the blood on the tabernacle and all the vessels of the ministry. He protected the ministry, tabernacle and everything that was present with the blood.

This scripture tells us that all things are purged with blood and if there wasn't any shedding of Jesus's blood, there would not be any remission (forgiveness). But thank God that Jesus shed His blood for all creation to be reconciled back to the Father.

Reason 7: Honoring communion (the blood) gives life to our daily lives and removes dead works from our conscience.

For the life of the flesh is in the blood: and I have given it to you upon the altar to make atonement for your souls: for it is the blood that maketh atonement for the soul (Leviticus 17:11).

When I think about honoring the blood in our daily walk, I think about the blood that runs through our natural body. The purpose of the blood flowing in our natural body is to keep the body alive. The blood of Jesus has the same operation: to keep our spiritual bodies (lives) alive.

When the Body of Christ honors the blood, life flows to that part of the body whether it is an individual life, home, job, church ministry or nation.

God told Moses that the blood was given to them upon the altar to make atonement for their souls. If we are dealing with anything in our "soul's" realm where our emotions, will and intellect are housed, we need to apply the blood of Jesus; the Lamb to that area.

How much more shall the blood of Christ, who through the eternal Spirit offered himself without spot to God, purge your conscience from dead works to serve the living God (Hebrews 9:14)?

Think about your personal altar (the place of prayer).The communion should be honored there every day. It is the very place where we can bring our souls to the altar and let the blood cleanse them.

In Leviticus 16:18, 19, the priest sprinkled the blood seven times around the altar. We can honor the blood seven times a day in our lives by:

1. Honoring the communion (the blood)
2. Reading about the blood
3. Writing about the blood
4. Hearing about the blood
5. Speaking about the blood
6. Singing about the blood
7. Meditating about the blood

We can honor communion in these seven ways and what it will do for us; for, it is the blood that makes atonement for our soul.

Confession: The blood forgives me of all my sin and I plead it upon my soul. The blood makes me whole.

In John 6, Jesus identifies himself spiritually as the bread of Heaven and is questioned of His natural lineage. Let's explore verses 49-58.

Verse [49]*Your fathers did eat manna in the wilderness, and are dead.* Jesus tells His nay sayers that their forefathers ate natural bread in the wilderness; but, even that did not keep them like spiritual food (the Word) can.

[50]*This is the bread which cometh down from heaven, that a man may eat thereof, and not die.* Jesus says that He is the living bread (spiritual food) that came down from heaven. We can partake of that spiritual food and not die.

[51]*I am the living bread which came down from heaven: if any man eat of this bread, he shall live forever: and the bread that I will give is my flesh, which I will give for the life of the world.* Jesus said that He is the "living bread" which came down from heaven. Anyone, who includes the whole world, who eats this bread and honors the cup of blessings, will live forever.

[52]*The Jews therefore strove among themselves, saying, How can this man give us his flesh to eat?* The Jews did not understand how Jesus was going to give His body to be eaten. They were unaware that Jesus was prophesying about giving up His life for the whole world to have life.

[53]*Then Jesus said unto them, Verily, verily, I say unto you, Except ye eat the flesh of the Son of man, and drink his blood, ye have no life in you.* Jesus said that if we do not partake of His flesh and drink of His blood we have no life in us. When we partake of His flesh and blood, life will be in us because the life of the flesh is in the blood. Even though Jesus was talking to the disciples, we can use the same principle today.

[54]*Whoso eateth my flesh, and drinketh my blood, hath eternal life; and I will raise him up at the last day.* When we eat Jesus' flesh (the bread) and drink His blood (the juice), we have the promise of eternal life. He also promised that He would raise up the people who honor the blood of the Lamb in the last day.

[55]*For my flesh is meat indeed, and my blood is drink indeed.* The flesh (body) of Jesus and the blood are what we should partake of to have life.

127

[56] *He that eateth my flesh, and drinketh my blood, dwelleth in me, and I in him.* When we eat of the bread and drink of the blood, (fruit of vine) we will dwell in Jesus. Then, Jesus will dwell in us because we honor His words concerning communion.

[57] *As the living Father hath sent me, and I live by the Father: so he that eateth me, even he shall live by me.* Jesus said the "living" Father sent Him; not a "dead" Father, Jesus lives by the Father's will; not His own. Jesus lived by His Father's instruction and He knew He was on an assignment. Jesus said that whoever eats from His life shall live through Him (His instruction) by honoring the communion.

[58] *This is that bread which came down from heaven: not as your fathers did eat manna, and are dead: he that eateth of this bread shall live forever.* Jesus emphasizes that the bread that came down from heaven is not the same bread that their forefathers had in the wilderness. When they ate the bread in the wilderness it did not last forever; but, when we eat of Jesus' bread, we shall live forever; because, He is the bread of life, not only in this life, but, the life to come.

Reason 8: Communion was ordained by our Lord and Savior Jesus Christ

Then came the day of unleavened bread, when the Passover must be killed (Luke 22:7).

Read Luke 22:7-22.

Jesus kept the instructions to memorialize the unleavened bread and the killing of the Passover Lamb. These instructions were given to the children of Israel (Exodus 12:13-27) and passed down to generations.

I like the word "Passover" because it means that anything dangerous or evil will pass over us. Also, it reminds me of Psalm 91:7,8 when David writes, "A thousand shall fall at thy side, and ten thousand at thy right hand; but it shall not come nigh thee. Only with thine eyes shalt thou behold and see the reward of the wicked." It is because of the Blood of the Lamb that we are protected and safe.

Verse [8]*And he (Jesus) sent Peter and John, saying, Go and prepare us the Passover that we may eat.*

Jesus <u>sent</u> Peter and John to prepare the Passover supper. This is an example of an apostolic anointing: Christ <u>sent</u> His disciples by two to prepare a place to eat.

[9] *And they said unto him, Where wilt thou that we prepare? And He said unto them, Behold, when ye are entered into the city, there shall a man meet you, bearing a pitcher of water; follow him into the house where he entereth in.*

Peter and John asked Jesus where to prepare the place for Passover supper. This is the instruction Jesus gave them:
1. He <u>sent</u> them into the city.
2. He said they would meet a man in the city.
3. The man they met would be bearing a pitcher of water.
4. The disciples needed to follow the man into the house that he entered in.

In this scripture, Jesus instituted the Lord's Supper in a man's house because the anointing flows from inside the house to the outside. Most issues we face begin in our homes concerning the husband, wife, children, creditors, decision-making and many other reasons. We probably make the most decisions in our homes. Even though Jesus did not institute communion in the Synagogue, during that time, we can still honor the blood at church because we are in covenant through the blood that Jesus shed for us.

And ye shall say unto the good man of the house, The Master saith unto thee, Where is the guest chamber, where I shall eat the passover with my disciples? And he shall shew you a large upper room furnished: there make ready (Luke 22:11, 12).

Jesus told His disciples to ask the good man, or head of the house, where the guestroom was so they could honor the Passover. Although, Jesus and the disciples were strangers to him, they ended up being a blessing to the man of the house. There are people that God sends into our lives who may have a message or may be a blessing to others for the purpose of the Kingdom. When the good man directed Jesus and the disciples to the upper room, Jesus told them to prepare the room for the Passover memorial.

In Acts 1:13, the apostles were waiting for the Holy Spirit in an upper room. In Acts 9, Dorcas was laid in an upper room when she died and was raised from her deathbed by Peter.

Could this have been the same upper room Jesus used to institute the Last Supper? The same room the Holy Spirit came into and filled lives with His Mighty Power because the blood and the Spirit bear witness in the earth? It could have even been the same upper room that Dorcas was brought back to life in when she laid dead. Notice I didn't say that it was, but it could have been because things change in the upper room.

Luke 22:13 *And they went, and found as he had said unto them: and they made ready the passover.*

The disciples were obedient and followed the instructions of Jesus without questioning when they prepared the Passover for the Master.

Luke 22:14-16: *And when the hour was come, he sat down, and the twelve apostles with him. And he said unto them, With desire I have desired to eat this passover with you before I suffer: For I say unto you, I will not any more eat thereof, until it be fulfilled in the kingdom of God.*

When it was time to institute the Lord's Supper, Jesus sat down with the 12 apostles (sent ones). He was going to send them to carry this ordinance through the Body of Christ. Thank God the Father, the gifts of the Apostles will be honored in these last days.

During the Passover meal in the house before He suffered, Jesus expressed how He felt to the Apostles. Usually, during a meal, sitting around a table, people will express how they feel about a situation.

In verse 16 Jesus said He would not eat of the supper any more until it is manifested in the kingdom of God. According to Revelation 19:9, the angel tells John to "...Write, Blessed are they which are called unto the marriage supper of the Lamb. And he saith unto me, these are the true sayings of God. "This scripture seems to foretell that we will be partaking of the Lord's Supper again in heaven.

> *And he took the cup, and gave thanks, and said, Take this, and divide it among yourselves: For I say unto you, I will not drink of the fruit of the vine, until the kingdom of God shall come. And he took bread, and gave thanks, and brake it, and gave unto them, saying, This is my body which is given for you: this do in remembrance of me. Likewise also the cup after supper, saying, This cup is the new testament in my blood, which is shed for you*
> (Luke 22:17-20).

It is very easy to follow the instructions Jesus gave about communion. This is how He did it:

1. He took the cup and gave thanks
2. He told the disciples to divide the cup among themselves
3. Jesus said He would drink the fruit of the vine when the kingdom of God comes (reign).
4. Jesus took the bread, gave thanks and broke it.
5. Jesus said "This is my body," which was given for us and told us to remember what He did.
6. Jesus and the disciples did communion during supper because the scripture says "Likewise also the cup after supper."
7. He let us know that the cup was a New Testament establishment in His blood that was shed for us.

Reason 9 *The Apostles observed the communion cup and the importance of honoring it from house to house.*

And they continued steadfastly in the apostles' doctrine and fellowship, and in breaking of bread, and in prayers (Acts 2:42).

The church continued to honor the blood. Jesus showed them how to pass it down through every generation. They were at the table when Jesus established it. Let's explore Acts 2: 43-47.

Verse [43]*And fear came upon every soul: and many wonders and signs were done by the apostles. [44]And all that believed were together, and had all things common;*

Things happen when all believers who have all things in common get together. Through the church's obedience to honor communion, fear came upon every (not some) soul, so much so that wonders and signs were done by the Apostles.

45-47*And sold their possessions and goods, and parted them to all men, as every man had need. And they, continuing daily with one accord in the temple, and breaking bread from house to house, did eat their meat with gladness and singleness of heart, Praising God, and having favor with all the people. And the Lord added to the church daily such as should be saved.*

The church sold their possessions and goods so that everyone would have enough. This is pure unselfishness and a willingness to share. They praised God and had favor with the people and the Lord daily added to the church because they stayed in the apostles' doctrine. Jesus <u>sent</u> them into the entire world to preach the gospel. John 15:7 says, "If ye abide in me, and my words abide in you, ye shall ask what ye will, and it shall be done unto you."

Since the apostles abided to Jesus' words about breaking the bread and drinking of the cup, this shows the church the importance of honoring communion in their houses and churches.

Let's look at I Corinthians 11:20-34

[20]*When ye come together therefore into one place, this is not to eat the Lord's Supper.*

Apostle Paul told the church at Corinth that when they come together in one place they are to honor the Lord supper with a right spirit. They should not see the Lord's Supper as a main meal; but, honor His death, burial, and resurrection.

[21]*For in eating every one taketh before other his own supper: and one is hungry, and another is drunken.*

The church was admonished to take the supper as a unit instead of individually.

[22]*What? Have ye not houses to eat and to drink in? Or despise ye the church of God, and shame them that have not?*

What shall I say to you? Shall I praise you in this? I praise you not.

Apostle Paul wanted to know if the people had houses to eat and drink in because they were causing shame and despising the church of God through their actions. Here fused to praise them for the disrespectful manner they chose to honor the Lord's Supper.

[23]For I have received of the Lord that which also I delivered unto you, That the Lord Jesus the same night in which He was betrayed took bread:

Paul received the Word from the Lord about how to remember the Lord's Supper and delivered that message to the body of Christ. He told them the story of how Jesus was betrayed the same night He was to go to the cross. He tells them that Jesus did not let the spirit of betrayal distract Him from His assignment. This shows us that right in the midst of betrayal or any other hindrance; through Jesus, we have the victory. John 16:33 tells us that Jesus has already overcome the world. According to Revelation 12:11, we overcome Satan by the blood of the Lamb and the word of our testimony; and we love not our life unto death.

[24]And when He had given thanks, He brake it, and said, Take eat: this is my body, which is broken for you: this do in remembrance of me.

Jesus gave thanks with the bread; then, broke the bread in the natural. Spiritually, Christ broke the spirit that tried to come on Him. He said take my anointing that was broken for you; and, remember, that I have overcome everything in the world. Remember me, He said, and remember what I did. Jesus is the example. Remember that you are an overcomer.

After Jesus gave thanks for the bread He honored the cup (the fruit of the vine) the same way. It was a reminder that the blood is a New Testament ordinance, and we are to drink it in remembrance of Him. We should remember what He did during tests and trials and honor the blood in the midst of our trials because of the established New Covenant. Whatever we remember and honor the bread and the blood for, He will cause us to get the victory in that area because He has overcame the world. We should be of good cheer because of the overcoming power we have by the blood of the Lamb.

[26] *For as often as ye eat this bread, and drink this cup, ye do shew the Lord's death till he come.*

Whenever we eat the bread and drink the cup, we are showing the Lord's victory over death until He returns to earth and take us to our heavenly home.

[27]*Wherefore whosoever shall eat this bread, and drink this cup of the Lord, unworthily, shall be guilty of the body and blood of the Lord.*

Jesus said that whoever does not know the power (meaning) of the bread that was broken and the blood that was shed for them will be guilty of the body and blood (death) of the Lord. It's best to seek God for the understanding of communion than to take it without understanding; because, you are at risk of bringing a spirit of guiltiness on your life.

[28]*But let a man examine himself, and so let him eat of that bread, and drink of that cup.*

Before honoring communion, we must examine ourselves. We should not be concerned with our neighbor; but, deeply look into own hearts to see if we have a good relationship to the Father and the Body of Christ. After we examine our own heart, we can eat the bread and drink of the cup.

²⁹⁻³⁰*For he that eateth and drinketh unworthily, eateth and drinketh damnation to himself, not discerning the Lord's body. For this cause many are weak and sickly among you, and many sleep.*

Weakness, sickness and death occur when there is no self-examination about what the bread and the blood has done and still does. The blood caused our sins to be forgiven and caused us to receive the love of the Father into our hearts. If you struggle in any area, repent before honoring communion and the blood of Jesus will cleanse.

³¹⁻³²*For if we would judge ourselves, we should not be judged. But when we are judged, we are chastened of the Lord, that we should not be condemned with the world.*

When we judge ourselves before the cup of blessings, others won't be able to judge us.

³³⁻³⁴*Wherefore my brethren, when ye come together to eat, tarry one for another. And if any man hunger, let him eat at home; that ye come not together unto condemnation. And the rest will I set in order when I come.*

Apostle Paul admonished the church at Corinth to make sure when they came together as a body to discern the Lord's supper; to tarry (wait) on one another, so that they can do it together and be on one accord. He goes on to say that, if they are hungry, they should eat at home before they honor the Lord's communion as a body. Paul did not want them to use the supper as a meal; but, as a celebration to signify the Lord's death, burial and resurrection. This way there won't be any condemnation, leaving God to put things in order when He returns.

And they continued steadfastly in the apostles' doctrine and fellowship, and in breaking of bread, and in prayers (Acts 2:41).

On the day of Pentecost when the Holy Spirit had come,

3,000 souls were saved and remained steadfast in what the apostles taught them about the communion cup. The apostles sat at the table with Jesus when He established communion. He instructed them to pass it on to the Body of Christ and the generations to come.

In verse 42 the apostles applied three things to their lives that they learned from Jesus:
1. Fellowship
2. Breaking of bread
3. Continual prayer

Verse 43 *And fear came upon every soul: and many wonders and signs were done by the apostles.*

Fear and change came upon every soul in the Upper Room and many wonders and signs were done by the apostles because they kept Jesus' teaching.

44-45 *And all that believed were together, and had all things common; and sold their possessions and goods, and parted them to all men, as every man had need.*

The people were on one accord. They became selfless with their possessions and goods. All that believed were gathered together and sold all they had to provide for every man's need. This reminds me of Ephesians 4:16 which says that every joint supplies. It didn't seem like any unbelievers were in the midst; and, if they were, they became believers.

46-47 *And they, continuing daily with one accord in the temple, and breaking bread from house to house, did eat their meat with gladness and singleness of heart, Praising God, and having favor with all the people. And the Lord added to the church daily such as should be saved.*

The people continued daily, not once a month, but daily in one accord in the temple. They broke bread from house to house, back and forth, with gladness and singleness of heart praising God and having favor with everyone. Their obedience caused the Lord to add to the church body daily.

What would the body of Christ look like if we were on one accord when we come together praising God? Would we have favor with all mankind? Only with God the Father is this possible. (Matthew 19:26).

Reason 10: We can honor communion to establish a relationship with the Father and for the needs of others.

But now in Christ Jesus ye who sometimes were far off are made nigh by the blood of Christ (Ephesians 2:13).

Adam and Eve committed high treason in the garden when they disobeyed the Lord's command; but, the blood of Christ Jesus brought us back into fellowship with the Father.

Through my personal time of communion with the Father, our relationship draws closer, especially when I honor communion according to the Word of God about something specific. For example, when I need peace about something, I use Colossians 1:20 which says,"…having made peace through the blood of his cross, by him to reconcile all things unto himself; by him, I say, whether they be things in earth, or things in heaven." I claim that scripture when I need peace in a relationship within the ministry, with a friend, on a job, or with relatives. It works every time. This can also be applied using any of the blood scriptures.

Like Mary said when the angel appeared unto her "Be it unto me according to thy Word."

If you ever want to be close to Christ, honor the communion in Jesus' name. We can do communion for our own errors and on the behalf of others. Hebrews 9:7 says, "But into the second went the high priest alone once every year, not without blood, which he offered for himself, and for the errors of the people:"

The high priest went into the holy of holies for five reasons:

1. **He always went in alone.** It's okay to honor the blood alone or with others.(Read Acts 2:41-47; I Corinthians 11:17-34)
2. **He went in yearly.** Though the priest went in yearly, remember we have the blood-bought right to honor the blood daily like the apostles did in the book of Acts. Just as we tell a loved one we love them daily; we daily want to express to Jesus how much we love and appreciate Him for shedding His blood for us.
3. **He didn't go in without the blood.** I encourage you to enter God's presence daily with the blood of the Lamb.
4. **He offers the blood for himself before the altar.** The priest realizes his sin and that the blood on his life would clean him first.
5. **He offers the blood on the behalf of the errors of the people.** As we honor the blood, we can also include others for a cleansing. We can lift up our families, nations, sins of omission, sins of commission, the presidents, governors, mayors, commissioners, Hollywood, schools, cities, states and many other people and see what the power of the blood will do for them in Jesus' name. Since it worked on a door in Egypt, it will work on anything.

Reason 11: *Communion gives us the blood-brought right to boldly (not timidly) enter the presence of the Father.*

This is the covenant that I will make with them after those days, saith the Lord, I will put my laws into their hearts, and in their minds will I write them; And their sins and iniquities will I remember no more (Hebrews 10:16-19).

The Father made a covenant (an agreement) with us that He will write His laws on our hearts and in our minds. The Father will not remember our sins, iniquities or the things we do wrong. His word inside us will bring about the change.

[18]*Now where remission of these is, there is no more offering for sin. Having therefore, brethren, boldness to enter into the holiest by the blood Jesus*

Since the Father does not remember our sins or iniquities, we can enter into the holiest because of the blood of Jesus. We don't have a sinful or guilty conscience, but a righteous conscience that gives us boldness to ask the Father what we will and to receive from His throne.

Reason 12: *Honoring communion gives us power to overcome the devil*

And they overcame him by the blood of the Lamb, and by the word of their testimony; and they loved not their lives unto the death (Revelation 12:11).

Prior to verse 11, the scriptures tell of a fight in the heavens between God and the enemy. Satan and his angels did not win because God prevailed and gave us the victory. We prevail over the enemy and any given situation by the blood of the Lamb and the words that we speak out of our mouth according to the Word of God.

The scripture said that they overcame Satan. We are not trying to overcome the enemy; we have already overcome the enemy by the blood and the Word of God.

When we overcome something there's no need to fight because victory is guaranteed.

I was dealing with a battle in my mind; but, as I was ironing clothes on a Monday night, the Holy Spirit showed me how people were victorious according to how the Holy Spirit ministered to them. The Holy Spirit is the teacher, not our experiences. There is nowhere in the Bible where we find that experience is the best teacher. The Word has examples that we learn from that are for our benefit placed a prayer cloth on my head that I had received from a ministry; I did as I was instructed; and, the battle in my mind ceased in the name of Jesus.

Before putting the prayer cloth on my head, I took communion. The peace of God that surpasses my understanding enlightened me to read a book from that ministry. I laid it down with the intentions of reading it later; but, the Holy Spirit and the blood agreed in one and brought revelation to do it then.

I Corinthians 2:8 say, "Which none of the princes of this world knew: for had they known it, they would not have crucified the Lord of glory."

The victory was won because none of the princes of this world knew what the blood of Jesus, the Lamb, would do for the whole world. That lets us know that devils don't know everything. Since they didn't know about the results of killing Jesus beforehand, they found out later that it was to their disadvantage to not have killed him, but to our advantage.

We are glad they didn't know; because, they weren't spiritual discerners. Hallelujah!!!!!

Now we have more things revealed unto us by the Spirit of God. Truly there is power in the blood!

> *It reaches to the highest mountain*
> *And it flows to the lowest valley*
> *The blood that gives us strength*
> *From day to day*
> *It will never lose its power.*

When we honor the communion cup in any area of our lives, we will receive answers to our prayers to give God the glory and the honor. PRAISE THE LORD!

If you would like to know how to receive Jesus Christ as Your Lord and Savior, feel free to contact me personally:

CONTACT INFORMATION
Post Office Box 90706
Columbia, SC 29290
Juanitaford27@yahoo.com
(404) 556-0867 Mobile

ACKNOWLEDGEMENTS

If you would like to invite Jesus into your heart today and begin a personal relationship with Him, read this short prayer aloud:

Repent of Your Sin

Father God, I recognize and admit that I am a sinner. The Bible says in 1 John 1:9 that if we confess of our sins, He is faithful and just to forgive us and cleanse us from all unrighteousness. Therefore, I repent of my sin, those that I can remember and those of which I am not aware. By saying these words, I receive Your forgiveness and I am in right standing with You.

Confess the Lord Jesus Christ
(Personalize)

Your Word says in Romans 10:9-10 that if I confess with my mouth the Lord Jesus and believe in my heart that You raised Him from the dead that I shall be saved. I believe Your Word and I make a quality decision to give my life to You today. As of this moment I AM SAVED! In Jesus' Name, Amen..

Date: _____

Time: _____

Begin a New Way of Life

Congratulations on the decision you have just made. Here's what you need to do next to begin living a victorious life in Christ.

1. Read the Bible and pray daily.
2. Find a church that teaches the Word of God clearly and accurately and with understanding.
3. Attend church services regularly and you will grow spiritually.

➤╱╲◄

Receive the Baptism of the Holy Spirit

To experience a closer walk with Christ, receive the baptism of the Holy Spirit with the evidence of speaking in tongues. Every born-again believer has the right to speak in tongues. The moment you were saved, the Holy Spirit moved into your heart. When you pray in tongues, you will experience more of God's power.

Luke 11:11-13 says that the Father will give us the Holy Spirit when we ask. In other words, we will receive the gift of speaking in tongues when we ask Him with confidence. "If a son shall ask bread of any of you that is a father, will he give him a stone? or if he ask a fish, will he for a fish give him a serpent? or if he shall ask an egg, will he offer him a scorpion? If ye then, being evil, know how to give good gifts unto your children; how much more shall your heavenly father give The Holy Spirit to them that ask him?" Therefore, ask, and you shall receive.

_____   Date of Salvation

_____   Holy Spirit Infilling

www.ingramcontent.com/pod-product-compliance
Lightning Source LLC
Chambersburg PA
CBHW060800050426

42449CB00008B/1469